READING THE BIBLE
AS CHRISTIAN SCRIPTURE:
Understanding the Writers' Use of Language

JAMES H. WARE JR.

Order this book online at www.trafford.com/08-0899
or email orders@trafford.com

Most Trafford titles are also available at major online book retailers.

Photography, cover/artwork and book design by James H. Ware, Jr.

Note for Librarians: A cataloguing record for this book is available from Library
and Archives Canada at www.collectionscanada.ca/amicus/index-e.html

Printed in Victoria, BC, Canada.

ISBN: 978-1-4251-8291-5 (sc)

*We at Trafford believe that it is the responsibility of us all, as both individuals
and corporations, to make choices that are environmentally and socially sound.
You, in turn, are supporting this responsible conduct each time you purchase a
Trafford book, or make use of our publishing services. To find out how you are
helping, please visit www.trafford.com/responsiblepublishing.html*

*Our mission is to efficiently provide the world's finest, most comprehensive
book publishing service, enabling every author to experience success.
To find out how to publish your book, your way, and have it available
worldwide, visit us online at www.trafford.com/10510*

Trafford
PUBLISHING® www.trafford.com

North America & international
toll-free: 1 888 232 4444 (USA & Canada)
phone: 250 383 6864 ♦ fax: 250 383 6804 ♦ email: info@trafford.com

The United Kingdom & Europe
phone: +44 (0)1865 487 395 ♦ local rate: 0845 230 9601
facsimile: +44 (0)1865 481 507 ♦ email: info.uk@trafford.com

10 9 8 7 6 5 4 3 2

To
Roy F. Melugin
and
Steve Stell:

Consummate scholars, colleagues,
and friends

ACKNOWLEDGEMENTS

I will be eternally grateful to Professor Roy Melugin and Professor Steve Stell. This book would not have turned out the way it has without their constructive criticism of the content and their personal interest in the project.

Our discussions and sometime arguments gave me clarity where I was vague in my own mind as to how to express what I wanted to say.

Numerous people helped me to get the book written. Professor Richard Hays suggested some reading with which I was not familiar *(N.T. Wright's, The Last Word, and The Art of Reading Scriptures, edited by Ellen F. Davis and Richard B. Hayes).* Paula Jonse typed and proofread the early draft copies. Eleanor Todd and Ethel Chamberlain proofread several chapters of the final draft. Ted Nickerson proofread and corrected the entire final copy.

I cannot thank them enough. I gave earlier drafts of the book to Dr. Victoria Jones, Dr Art Crosswell, and Dr. Lindsay Moffett for their comments and revised parts of the book that may have been misleading. If there are errors in the book or misleading passages, I must take responsibility for them completely.

I always have to thank my wife Emma for letting me take so much time away from doing things together. She has been both patient and encouraging.

All scripture citations are taken from The Revised Standard Version of the Bible

CONTENTS

Acknowledgements iv

Preface 1

Chapter I   The Semantics of the Scriptures 6

   I. Referential Meaning 7

   II. Significance 21

   III. Consequential Meaning 25

   IV. Summary 27

Chapter II   Significance: Truth and Witnesses 33

   1. Authentication and Verification 33

   2. A Short History of *Truth* in the Western World 35

   3. Biblical Processes for Authenticating or

     Verifying Statements 38

     A. The Words of a Prophet 39

     B. Accounting for Claims and Counter Claims 42

     C. Witnesses 45

Chapter III   Super-session and Significance 53

Chapter IV   Consequential Meaning and The Language of Precedents 72

Chapter V   Consequential Meaning and Performative Language 92

   1. Consequential Meaning in the Scriptures 92

   2. Consequential or Performative Meaning 97

   3. Consequential Language and Biblical Usage 99

     A. Constitutive Language 100

     B. Bonding Statements 105

     C. Expressive Statements 107

     D. Exalting Statements 109

     E. Transforming Statements 110

     F. Comforting and Blessing Statements 113

     4 Conclusion 115

About the Author 117

PREFACE

This project was begun about fifteen years ago while I was still teaching at Austin College. A number of my students who had been to seminary and were pastoring churches asked me for materials to help them interpret Christian Scriptures in preparation for preaching. One of the common themes they expressed was that the available commentaries and other biblical study materials did not address their needs as pastors. When I asked them to elaborate, most of them said that the material which they had, addressed academic rather than parish issues.

I took the issue up with my colleague Professor Roy Melugin, and the two of us spent several years together agreeing and disagreeing on what route to take. We were joined by Professor Steve Stell, who was also teaching at Austin College. As time went by the three of us began to see that it would be difficult, if not impossible, for us to come out with a strong consensus. Someone's point of view was going to be distorted.

For most of my teaching career I have taught Comparative Religions, the History of Philosophy, and Philosophy of Language with an emphasis on hermeneutics. One of my earlier projects was a comparative study of the use of language in Japanese, Jodo Shin Shu Buddhism, Korean Folk Religions, and Confucianism. When I taught the History of Western Philosophy, one of the subjects, which I found missing in that discipline, was an understanding of how language was used in non-Greek cultures. Hellenic language usages were well explored, but the language of both the Old and New Testaments, with the exception of logos theory, were not covered. Modern discussions of religious language both in philosophy and theology usually focused on how to talk about God, logos theory, or how to talk about the Christian faith in modern scientific terms. I thought that it would be interesting to look at how language was used in the Bible itself. It seemed anachronistic to me to apply theories of language to interpret the Bible that were not part of the usage pattern of the people who wrote the Bible and first used the Bible as Scripture.

I started out trying to determine the semantic understandings which underlie the text. This was the least difficult task. First, the biblical use of language presupposes a referential meaning. The referential understanding that underlies biblical language was Pre-enlightenment, and very closely akin to the work of Ludwig Wittgenstein and Charles Peirce. Words mean the way they are used to mean. Second, the Bible incorporated as meaning not only the referential use of language, but also the issue of significance. The question of significance is almost universally applicable to a text, "What difference does it make?" I was surprised when I began to realize that the biblical writers' use of older texts within new contexts meant a change in the significance of the text. There is no literature, as far as I am aware of it, either in the philosophy of language or in hermeneutics which deals with *significant meaning*. It was clearly inseparable from representations and referential uses of language, but a move from one context to another often changed the significance of what has been said. The third type of semantics used in the Bible, which is also not separable from referential and significant meaning, is consequential meaning or the *force* of what is said in a given situation. J. L. Austin and others have developed that notion in contemporary philosophy of language, but I was introduced to it much earlier by biblical scholars like H. Wheeler Robinson and Eric Rust.

Once I got into the semantic uses of language in the Bible, I began to look for the biblical use of *truth*. I discovered that the common understanding of *truth* as the correspondence of language to the reality to which it refers is used in the Bible, but that there were more ways to authenticate and establish a statement than trying to discover if its referent corresponded to the normal use of the words involved. At least two other criteria of *authenticity* are used. A statement was established in the mouth of two examined witnesses, and the words of a prophet were authenticated as they came to pass. These two understandings of authenticity and establishment are often overlooked in contemporary circles. Although we recognize four types of *truth*: representational, pragmatic, coherent, and existential, we pay little attention to other forms of authenticity.

The study of how language was authenticated in the Bible led me to look at how later writers of Scripture used earlier texts to authenticate their understanding of a given situation. I began to realize that arguments and statement of right and wrong were often determined by earlier precedents. This in turn led me to look at how conflicting statements and later statements were authenticated. Biblical jurisprudence did not rest on universal principles or laws, but on the adjudication of precedents.

Finally, I tried to show some of the different forms of consequential language that were used in the Bible. Much of this work was an expansion of "Not With Words of Wisdom" which I published over twenty years ago.

Every thing I have written for this project has been derived from the language of the Bible. Where I have cited sources, I have done so as secondary back up, to let the reader know that I was acquainted with the subject matter as it has been discussed in the academy, and to provided them a resource for further study.

I have tried to stay within the biblical framework which I perceived as necessary for the life of the Church. I have studiously avoided arguments from contemporary philosophy, theology, hermeneutics, and the social sciences to make my points. It is a matter of credo for me to examine a linguistic topic within the context in which it is put forward and to refrain from using explanatory categories from other contexts. My training in philosophy, theology, hermeneutics, comparative religions, and biblical studies has led me to that conclusion. Categories that are alien to the language usage of a given community distort the message that is implicit in the language of a text written in the writer's community. I think that it is self evident that Buddhist and Confucian categories, when used to interpret the Bible, distort Jewish-Christian writings. It is no less true of the interpretive categories we use in our post-Enlightenment disciplines.

How was this to help the pastor with biblical exegesis? First, and foremost, with careful reading one had many, if not all, of the exegetical tools that are needed in the Bible itself. It was not necessary for a pastor to become an expert in contemporary hermeneutics or to keep up with the debates that were going on in the academy. Second, the pastor's message would be grounded in the language of the Bible. His task would NOT be to translate the Bible into modern idiom so much as to teach his congregation how to read the Bible and encourage them to apply it to the current circumstances.

I ask the reader to read carefully. This book does not approach understanding of the Scripture in the same way that most of us have been taught in the academy. What we have learned about the Bible in the past fifty years is basically out of an historical critical set of presuppositions. We have all tried to make the Bible more intelligible to the modern world by restating our understanding of the Bible in contemporary terms. The historical critical method has been helpful, but our attempts to make the Bible relevant to the contemporary reader have for the most part reduced the Scriptures to mere history rather than the Word of God. This book to some degree is an open break with our recent past, but not without appreciation for what we have learned from historical criticism and more recently Post Modernism. It is, however, a break with these two traditions, and an attempt to understanding of the Bible in the use of its own language. I hope that the reader learns to understand the use of language by the Biblical writers in order to gain a deeper access to the Bible as Christian Scripture, and thereby grow in the knowledge of the Word of God.

Some scholars would say that what has been stated in these earlier paragraphs is a capitulation to Fundamentalism and Fideism, but they are wrong. Throughout this exploration of biblical language there has been the assertion that the language of the Bible is that of a world-view different from the contemporary world of modern science. This determination was made on rational bases, i.e., a comparison of the language of the worldview of modern science and the language of Scripture. Fundamentalists do not recognize this distinction. They hold that there is no difference between the language of the modern scientific world and biblical language, and where there appears to be a difference that biblical language should prevail over scientific language.

Fideism would hold that biblical language should be simply accepted on faith. We have tried to show in this book how biblical language is used in developing personal and social identity. We have done so by looking phenomenologically at how in fact biblical language is actually used, and what the consequence of using biblical language has on the lives of those who use it for religious ends.

If biblical language is to be used at all in our Christian understanding of ourselves and the Church, it must be done with the clear understanding that it does not function like modern scientific language. It is representational only because it functions as transformational and consequential language requires it to be so. Just as the statements, "I love you," or "Thou shalt not commit adultery," can not be verified empirically, yet serve as bonding statements and prescriptive statements, biblical language has its own context of meaningfulness. It has its own meaningful use in the formation of the identity of Christians and the Church that is phenomenologically recognizable. It is not a question of biblical authority as claimed by Fundamentalism, nor is it a matter of blind faith as Fideists might insist. The language of the Scriptures is neither the language of modern science nor a supernatural language that can not be studied phenomenolically. It is the language of *its own worldview* which we can understand by examining it within the coherence of that worldview, though we may do it poorly.

CHAPTER I

The Semantics of the Scriptures

No where in the Scriptures is there a formal statement of the semantic understandings underlying the texts. The Bible does not tell us how words mean. It must be extrapolated from the use of language in the texts themselves. In the Scripture here are innumerable clues as to how meaning is expressed in the use of language; but there is no systematic formulation of a semantic theory or theories. There are no psychological terms, such as *idea, impression, icon, index, signal, sign, mental images, etc.* that are used in modern philosophy to refer to the meaning of a words as they are purported to occur in our minds. In fact there is no teaching that the meaning of words occurs in our heads at all. Sometimes meaning is located in a person's heart, but this is not uniformly the case. As we shall see the meaning of a word or phrase in the Bible may be completely independent of our faculties and senses. There is no epistemological theory stated in the texts which tells us how the readers and writers of the texts understood how words communicated or how language conveys meaning.

Also, there is no normative way set out to go about understanding words, signs, or other forms of communication. Various forms of communication are simply there in the text and vary from one occasion to another as to how they are used.

In this chapter I want to describe three concepts of meaning as they have bearing on the language of the Scripture.

We can analytically identify (distinguish in thought, if not in reality) at least three senses of the word *meaning* which are relevant to the task of interpreting the Bible: (1) referential meaning, (2) significance, and (3) consequential meaning. In the interpretation of the Bible for the life of the Church these three senses of *meaning*, are inseparably bound together and are interdependent in the texts. They can not be separated in actual language usage. However, any one of them, or several of them, can be identified as the focus of a given act of communicating. We can separate them out from one another analytically, that is, we can separate them out in thought as we attempt to identify how language works. Our differentiation of them is one way to understand how a given communication *means.*

Referential meaning includes the broadest and most problematic set of activities used in communication. Referential meaning is what we in the modern world normally associate with the term *meaning*. When a word, term, sign, symbol, or phrase calls to our attention to something other than itself, we say the term refers to that which it calls to mind. What ever it calls to our attention is its referent. When we learn a language, we learn the association which our language community makes between a given word, sign, or symbol, etc. and its referent. An agreement, tacit or otherwise, has been accepted by the language community to use a given word, sign, or symbol, to communicate a given referent.

The referential meaning of a term gives us the conceptual information or content of a discourse in a given context. In ordinary language almost every word can be taken to refer to a number of different referents. The context in which the word is used gives the immediate sense of a word. The word, it self, is a matter of convention, i.e., the use of the community informs us which referent is appropriate to a term in the context of a given discourse. With some notable exceptions, which we will deal with later on, there is no necessary connection between a given word and its referent. When we learn to use a language to communicate, we learn how a community uses a word or statement within a given context. Consequently, in different communities we have different languages. If we go to a dictionary or a lexicon, we are looking for the referential meaning of the term in question within a given language community.

Going to a dictionary or lexicon is often the beginning of a process of determining the referential meaning of a given word or statement. Dictionaries and lexicons record the common referential use of terms, but the task of determining the referential meaning of a specific term often requires considerably more effort. For example, the act of translating a text from one language to another is more than simply finding a proper word substitution. It involves the skill of functioning within the language conventions of two separate communities of communication and being able to contextualize the translation so that it does not lose its original referential meaning. This, at times, can be very difficult when two communities configure their world or their language differently; for example, when verbs are used to express time in completely different ways.[1]

There are at least four factors which impact the way in which language refers to reality. The first consideration of any referential meaning is ***context***. No word, name or statement, apart from the context in which it is used, has a privileged relationship to a referent. The context of a given word is determined not only by the sentence in which it appears, but also within the entire event and discourse of which it is a part. The word "eye" can be used to refer to an eye of a needle, an organ of vision, the center of a storm, etc. "Eye" can be used as a noun or a verb. It can be used to refer to objective reality, and it can be use to refer to a judgment such as, "John has an eye for that sort of thing."[2]

The second feature of referring is the ***manner*** in which a sign or a symbol calls forth its referent. Signs and symbols can be used to point to a referent, name a referent, picture a referent, suggest a referent, "cause a referent to stand in openness," differentiate a referent, be an ontological part of its referent, etc. The medium of a communication impacts the referential process and content. Writing, speech, pictures, touch, body language, etc, can influence the referential meaning of a communication. Different types of referential meaning may require different media to communicate them appropriately.

Most people live under the illusion that language replicates the reality to which it refers and that all referential functions of language are like naming living beings and physical objects. They think of referring in literalistic terms, i.e., all language names objective reality on a one-to-one basis like when we name living things, physical objects, and their characteristics.

Much the same understanding is expressed in Genesis 2:19-20 when man is looking for a help mate, God observes what humans call each living thing; and, what humans call them is subsequently their name. In the Scriptures after the flood narratives, as humans began to migrate toward the east, culturally develop, and make brick, they decided to make a name for themselves; they decide to become self important. They began to build a city with a tower that reached heaven. At that time, according to the text, the whole earth had one language and few words. There was only one people. God confused their language, and they gave up on building the city which they had named Babel. Since there was no longer a single language, there was no longer a single people; and, humans were scattered over the face of the earth (Gen. 11: 1-9).

In these early Genesis passages it is stated that names were given to living things in a rather conventional manner; human created names for objects. But there are three other situations in the Scripture that give names a more ontological connection to that which is named.

(1) The first of these is connected to the practice of levirate marriage. In Deuteronomy 25:5-10 we read that when a man died, his brother was responsible to marry the decease's widow; and the first child of the second marriage would bear the original husband's name in order that his name not be blotted out of Israel. The practice is attested to in the fourth chapter of Ruth when Boaz, acting as the responsible kinsman, buys the deceased Elimelect's property from his widow, Naomi. Included in his purchase is Naomi's daughter in law Ruth, who is also widowed. Boaz asserts the right of a responsible kinsman and marries Ruth. The first child under this marriage "perpetuates the name of the dead (man) in his inheritance, that the name of the dead may not be cut off from among his brethren and the gate of his native place" (Ruth 4:9-17). In these passages the name given to the child carries on something of the decease's existence in a subsequent generation. The child's name is more than a simple designation; it continues the presence of the deceased among his people. The connection of the name and the named is almost substantive. By keeping the deceased name alive Boaz and Ruth act as redeemers of the family name.

(2) The second substantive notion of a name is best seen in the commandment, "You shall not take the name of the Lord your God in vain, for the Lord will not hold him guiltless who takes His name in vain." (Ex. 20:7). This commandment has often been interpreted in the light of Lev.24:10-12 where, in a dispute with another Israelite, a man blasphemes the Name and curses. Moses proceeds to have the blasphemer of God's name stoned. The meaning of the commandment, however, is more profound. It directs Israel not to take on God's name in vain, i.e. to be an apostate or a hypocrite. To take on a name is similar to the modern day practice when a woman marries and she takes her husbands name as her own. Israel was commanded not to take on God's name as His people, and not live accordingly. In the commandment God's name is more substantive than a conventional name. It requires that the person live up to the quality of life associated with the name.

(3) The third example of a non-conventional name is recorded in the New Testament accounts of Jesus' name. In Acts 2:38 Peter admonishes those who hear him at Pentecost, "Repent and be baptized every one of you in the name of Jesus Christ for the forgiveness of your sin: and you shall receive the gift of the Holy Spirit." To be baptized in the name of Christ was to take on that name as a designation for one's selfhood. Christians were to take on the name of Jesus Messiah as their identity. As in the Old Testament, a person was to live worthily of the name he had taken on and by which he was called to be a child of God. In The Book of Acts there is no other name under heaven given whereby one is saved other than Jesus' name. (Acts 4:12). Requests and prayers were to be offered in Jesus' name (John 14:13). In each of these cases, as in others which are similar, the name of Jesus Messiah functions in much the same fashion as the person of Jesus Messiah himself. To use Jesus' name is to affect his presence.

God's name and the name of Jesus Messiah function differently in the Scriptures than any other names. These names were thought to function as the referent to which they pointed. To call on the name of the Lord was to call on God Himself. To take on the name of Jesus Messiah was to live in substantial union with the Messiah. The relationship between God's name and God Himself was not just a referential tie, but an identity of name and referent. There is an anomaly in the case of the name for God. In Exodus 3: 13-15 God tells Moses that, when he is asked what God's name is and who has sent him, he should reply, "The Lord, the God of your Fathers, the God of Abraham, the God of Isaac, and the God of Jacob, has sent me to you: this is my name for ever, and thus I am remembered throughout all generations." There are many other names in the Old Testament used to designate God: El Shaddai, El Bethel, El Roy, El Elon etc. These latter names seem to be conventional within the contexts that they are used, and are seemingly not substantively used in relationship to God as are Yahweh or Elohim.

In the Scriptures it is not uncommon to find human beings changing their names as their relationship with God changes. Abram's name is changed to Abraham; Jacob's name to Israel; Saul's name to Paul; Peter's name from Cephas to Simon or Peter; etc.

Often a person's name changed with their role within the Scripture's narratives. But in no case did a human's name function as the name for God or the name for Jesus Messiah. The change of name marked a distinction between the person before the person is called to a mission and what he is later because of his mission. These name changes seem to have been part of the conventions of the community at that time. Only with the name of God and Jesus is the naming process more than a conventional use of a term to refer to a given referent.

The accounts in Genesis shows very little understanding of how we refer to nonphysical realities such as abstractions, universals, mathematical functions, possible realities, imagined realities, transcendent realities, and ethical and interpersonal realities. This does not mean that the writers of the Scriptures did not have names for some of these referents; they simply did not develop them.

Biblical language uses almost all the literary genre that we use in modern languages. It is some times clear and at other times more problematic when they use univocal language and equivocal language to communicate their messages. Poems, songs, verse, stories, parables, riddles, analogies, metaphors, and apocalyptic language are all part of the usage of the biblical writers. The biblical writers were not limited to univocal prepositional statements.

Existential reality, the reality which most of us intuit both as our subjective and objective world, the shared world in which we live and interact with one another, is particularly constituted by realities which are abstractions, generalizations, laws, social and scientific paradigms, and interpersonal attitudes and relationships. Justice, faith, hope, and love are as much a part of our existential world as are chairs, tables, red, white, blue, sweet, loud, and rough.

Terms which refer to our existential world do not need to have as their referents physical objects. The nature of the referent's reality is a separate issue from the referential meaning of a statement. For example, the referential meaning of, "The bell in the little red school house is ringing" is not dependent on whether this is a description of a physical event or whether the statement is part of a fictitious novel. The referential meaning is different only in context.

The referential meaning of an analogical statement or metaphor is merely a complex way to refer to a given referent by using the similarity and difference of one referent to refer to another. When we state, "He is acting like a bull in a china shop." The referential meaning operated on two levels; it uses the prima facie reference to an animal's behavior to refer analogically to a human's behavior. It employs a systematic ambiguity which is understood in a given language community. The fact that there may never have been a bull in a china shop is irrelevant. The metaphysical state of the prima facie referent may determine HOW a statement is understood, i.e., its context of meaning, but it does not determine the referentiality of the statement. The referential meanings of statements are determined by the community of the language users who employ them to refer directly or analogically to a referent or referents. Analogies and metaphors refer in the same equivocal manner as other equivocal genre that a language community uses.[3]

Some types of statements are systematically ambiguous, i.e., they have a surface referent and a depth referent. Fables, parables, and myths have a surface referent but also carry a depth referent, a moral principle or teaching. Puns are systematically ambiguous, that is, they play on ambiguity, the double or triple referential meaning of a term. Apocalyptic language has a surface referent, and the depth referent is hidden except to those who have the key to read it. Even some works of fiction, such as *Uncle Tom's Cabin*, have surface referential meaning which refers to a depth referent, i.e., the evils of slavery. The fact that a statement may have more than one referent which is meaningful depends upon the conventions of the community which uses the language where systematic ambiguity is employed.

Often the question of referential meaning has hung on the question whether the referent for a given word or statement is *"real."* There are those who question whether one is making any sense when the words used refer to "non-existent" referents. Actually this is a metaphysical question about the nature of a referent, not a semantic issue about the nature of language to refer. When we use language to communicate, we communicate various forms of reality, fiction, abstraction, etc. All language which communicates within a community of users has referential meaning. The issue as to whether the referents are real, fictional, imaginary, or abstraction, etc., does not change the function of language to refer to it. How referents exist or do not exist is not a semantic issue; the semantic issue is how a community uses language to communicate those references which it chooses to identify. We use all sorts of genre to communicate different forms of references. The genre we use is part of the context which a given word or a statement its referential meaning and sometimes gives us a good idea as to the metaphysical status of its referent.

The ability to use words to refer to that which is not immediately present or that which currently does not exist in the basis for writing history, repeating traditions, projecting the future, stating moral ideals, voicing one's hope, and stating one's objectives. The fact that we can talk about that which is not immediately present, and that which is merely possible, is implicit in our temporality as human beings. Of course, this same ability occurs is the use of imagination to create fiction and entertainment. Each of these functions of referring has its own set of rules which we habituate and which are intelligible to the person who learns to use them in a given language community.

The manner in which a given type of referent is called forth by language depends on the community of language users. The same terms or statements can be used to refer to a genus or universal concept or be applied to an individual member of a set or class. Grammatically and logically the same term can be used both as the subject of a sentence or can be used to describe an object in a statement. All of these referential processes depend upon the communication rules and the practices of the community in which they are employed and the manner in which we have learned them.[4] Regardless of the community, the process which is being used to communicate a referent (either real or imaginary) is essential for there to be meaning; without the communities accepted processes there is no referential meaning.[5]

In summary, how a term designates, opens up its referent, or is associated with its referent depends upon the manner in which the community of users of the language have determined either consciously of unconsciously that a term will function. When we refer to something we may be using language to differentiate it from the world in which it is imbedded. We may be employing it as Martin Heidegger put it, "to cause something to stand in openness." It may involve the separation of the referent from its background. It may place the referent in the foreground of our attention.[6]

Naming a thing may differentiate its being or bring its uniqueness into focus as Derrida claims. Most people think of a word as "pointing to" its referent, that is as denoting or connoting a referent. Others have suggested that the relationship between a word and its referent is a matter of conditioning and habit.

The third factor involved in the referring process is the fact that we can **create** distinctions in language which do not otherwise exist. We can analytically separate minds and bodies, and we can perform reductionisms which void the distinctions that have been made previously. It is possible to change from one set of categories to another and use those category distinctions to formulate new solutions or create new problems. The history of science is a clear example of how we adopt new paradigms and make paradigm shifts to deal with the same world which we have dealt with at previous times and other places.[7]

Every community which uses a given language has a way of going about representing the world in their language. In every language the way in which we organize the world has generalizations and processes which are accepted either consciously or tacitly as the normal way of looking at that which makes up our experiences. Communities create and sustain them. These organizational generalizations are there for the users to order the world of which we are conscious, and they provide a common basis for communicating and living in our world. Getting an education is basically learning to use a language or system of symbols to order our experiences. Language makes it possible for us to communicate our understanding of the world around us, and it allows us to solve problems without actually using the world of objects and relationships.

Usually, the verbal expressions of these ordering generalizations or paradigms are central to the way that a community intellectually responds to that which they experience and organizes that experience into a *world*. Humans can and do build their communities on these paradigms. When the models and paradigms are well in place in the communities that use them to understand and react in the world, they can be used to create new and real differences in the world in which we live. For example: when a new experience does not fit into the language categories that we have been using, we add terms and new categories to help us to understand and re-spond to the *reality* they shape. Some of these paradigms are more primary than others. The category and paradigm shifts which we make in language become a part of the community's mode of understanding and expression, and they generate not only a worldview, but can be used to generate part of our *reality*. As new paradigms become indigenous to our languages, they transform our existing understanding and behavior. Sometimes old para-digms fade away or are disposed of and are no longer use to structure the world which we refer to in our language. The use of new paradigms creates new intellectual artifacts; change our attitudes; reshape our institutions; help to evolve new relationships; create new art forms, technologies, and science. What is created when a paradigm shift occurs is not merely a dif-ference in the way the *world* is perceived, but differences in the features of the *world* itself that can be observed and studied. These differences some-times are simply subjective, i.e. in the minds of the community members which employ them; but, they can also become objectified so that we can study and examined them in themselves. They can even take on a life of their own, and set us into motion to discover new experiences, institution, and realities.

The language of the Bible not only construes the world differently than the language used in modern societies, it configures *reality* differently. The contemporary common world, of which we all are an immediate part, is not uniform either diachronically or synchronically. "*Reality*," and the way that we understand it through language, often changes over a period of time. It is possible to be engaged with two different paradigms of *reality* simultaneously. An object or event experienced in the language of one *world* is not always experienced in the same way in another. Existentiality joins all of us at the hip, as it were; we share a great deal in common regardless of the time and place we live. But some of the particulars of our existentiality are disconnected from the past and from other contemporary groups. The "*world*" of the Bible has many paradigms that are the same as the modern world of the twenty first century. But it is also has models and paradigms which are radically different. The Bible can not be read intelligently if one expects the *world* of the Bible to be the same as that of the *world* of modern science. A process of interpretation, i.e. a hermeneutics, which tries to translate features of the Biblical world into the language of modern day scientific and critical paradigms, is one way that we have tried to bridge the gap between the two *worlds*. Unfortunately this process appears to be doomed to failure in key circumstances. There is just too much difference between the Biblical *world* and the scientific *world*; although the two systems occur in the same space-time continuum.

The modern *world* in which we live is very diverse; there is no one set of paradigms which will include every aspect of it. We do not live in a "universe" that is understandable through one set of paradigms. We live in a "multiverse" of differing paradigms and therefore multiple symbolic systems. In fact, in the Anglo-American symbolic systems of the twenty first century we live in several "*worlds*" simultaneously. It is not until someone calls our attention to the fact that our understanding, which is taught to us, includes a wide range of different models and paradigms that we recognize the discontinuity of our thoughts both within our societies and within our own understanding.

For example: there are some things which we refer to using mathematical paradigms which simply can not be put into empirical language. The square-root of minus one functions in a mathematical world, but can not function in an empirical world. Almost everyone understands when it is said that the average American family has 2.5 children that this is numerically speaking and can not be demonstrated as an empirical fact. There are no .5 children! When we designate a person's intelligence quotient with numbers, we know that we are not speaking of something that is a physical reality, but one that is generated by mathematical comparisons.

The world of mathematics and the world of sense data do not exist or operate in the same manner. The same is true of reality viewed from a microscopic or macroscopic perspective. On the microscopic level everything is in motion; nothing is literally stationary as it is in our every day *world* of experience. The macroscopic *world* does not seem to operate like either the microscopic or everyday *world*. How the *world* is understood differs depending on the conceptual framework used to study it. Some phenomena of light are understood as waves; whereas other phenomena are best interpreted as particle. Regardless of which paradigms we use our continuum is the same, although the experienced particulars are different. We function in everyday life with different paradigms at the same time, and recognize that they are not commensurate with one another and cannot be used to replace one another. These anomalies are part of our "multiverse" *world*.

It has long been recognized that faith and reason can exist side by side in an individual and in a community. Some people claim that there is no real difference between the two sets of paradigms. But others have recognized that the two sets of paradigms are different and must be systematically treated as related to one another one way or another, but not reduced to one or the other. In reading the Bible it is a poor understanding that wishes to reduce the Biblical *world* to our own or our own into the Biblical *world*. The worshiping community with its paradigms and traditions exist side by side with our scientific and analytical world, and we live in both. We have to learn how to allow them to function and produce that which is good for us out of each context of our understanding. That which holds together the world of the past and the present world are the continuums of experience, memory, persistent artifacts, records of events, and written histories.

In the twentieth century biblical scholarship has tried to use contemporary intellectual tools to understand Biblical language. The language of the Bible, its paradigms and organizational concepts, are different from the paradigms of modern science. The attempt to restate Biblical language in terms of the intellectual language of the twentieth century has worked very poorly because the defining paradigms are very different in critical ways. Attempts to demythologize Biblical language, i.e. to recast the key paradigms of Biblical language in twentieth century terms has simply failed because the consequence of using modern paradigms to explain Biblical concepts transforms Biblical categories into something that they are not. There is no question that the task has been well meaning, but there is no way to reduce the Biblical language and its paradigms to modern language and its paradigms. It does violence to the Bible to take the terminology and Biblical paradigms as if they were myths or metaphors. Contemporary biblical studies do violence to the paradigms and thought patterns in the Bible when they treat them as "untrue" or equivocal statements for modern readers.

There may be myths and metaphors and other forms of equivocal statement in the Scriptures, but they can only properly be understood within the framework of the paradigms that shape the Biblical worldview and not our own. The writers of the Bible lived within the same space-time continuum that we do, but their way to understand the world is different from our modern scientific worldview. They used different paradigms to communicate what they have to say about the *world;* yet they were describing the same continuum which we try to live in. Consequently, the modern interpreter's task is to teach the Biblical paradigms and narratives to a community which has very little appreciation of those paradigms.

Philip Jenkins in *The New Faces of Christianity: Believing the Bible in the Global South* has demonstrated that readers of the Bible in the Third World have a much easier time appropriating the Biblical world view than those of us who live in a scientific and technological world. Their paradigms are closer to those of the Scripture than the paradigms of scientific-technological world.[8] Whether or not we who live in a scientific technological world have lost the ability to work with two set of paradigms for the world is a problem we must face, if we want to understand the Bible as it is written.

The desire to live under one set of linguistic paradigms seems to be part of our human need to live in a unified world. In fact we do not. Anyone who has attempted to describe the world mathematically can tell you in no uncertain terms that there will be a difference between a mathematically modeled world and a world organized by sense data. Because we are simultaneously taught both systems of organizing our world, we are able to keep the relationship between a mathematically ordered world and a world organized by sense experience in perspective with one another. This is not true of the language of modern science and Biblical language. In our Enlightenment Age we tend to give precedence to the language and paradigms of science over those of the Bible. In order to bring about a synthesis of the two, we are conditioned by our academic experiences to believe that one or the other must be reduced to a single system. The issue is not new. The relationship of the language of faith to the language of reason has been a problem through out the history of the Church. H. Richard Niebuhr wrote *Christ and Culture* in 1951 where he attempted to show that there have been as many as five different ways the Church has attempted to bring together the language of faith and the language of culture.[9] Although Niebuhr is not talking specifically about Biblical language and the language of the twentieth century, the categories are still relevant.

Referential meaning is the ground for comparison between two different systems of narrating about the world. Anyone dealing with the referential meaning of the language of the Bible for the modern world will have to deal with the way in which that meaning interacts with the language of modern science. The position taken in this work is that the two language systems, though very disparate in their understanding of the world, are nevertheless necessary and complimentary to one another. The referential meaning of both the language of the Bible and the language of Modern Science must be contextualized with the significance and consequential meaning of each as they are used in the processes of life, and in the search for a meaningful life in the world in which we live.

We may wish that the universe was explainable in one set of language paradigms that are both synchronic and diachronic universe. There are things, objects, places, and even events which can be described in every place and time. But the explanations of these objects, places, and events do not remain the same either synchronically or diachronically. In this sense universe is not uniform. The world of which the Biblical writers speak is the same world of objects as that in which we live, but it is different in scope and organization from the contemporary world. The commandments, and narratives refer to the same world as that in which we live, but the scope of what is communicated does not easily mesh with our "worldview" and the world which is created by our paradigms. For example, the Gospel writers referred to the same existential world in which we all live; but the scope of that world includes divine intervention on a regular basis. This is not the same as our contemporary "world view" of the world in which divine intervention is problematic. Therefore, there is a need for interpretation.

Consequently, when we think of the process by which words refer to their referents there is no simple process of replication taking place. Communication and dialogue are complex operations in which word, sentences, and discourse reflect their referent in different way with regard to their context of usage. The manner in which they are used to refer and to be understood is a skill which is always more or less proficient and therefore imperfect. Learning to read or speak with differing paradigms is a skill learned from the community to which the language belongs.

The fourth feature of referential meaning deals with how words refer to the **aspect** of their referents. When we refer to something with language we always refer to some aspect of the referent and never reproduce or replicate the referent in its completeness. Language is not a process of Xeroxing referents. Language is always less than that which it represents. Language is a human shortcut to deal with "reality." But as it refers to that which is not itself; it is always less than that to which it refers. Not to understand this is to fall into assumptions which seriously mislead the understanding of referentiality. This is what literalists often do. Whether we take the words or statements declaratively, prescriptively, interrogatively, propostionally, poetically, fictionally, analogically, metaphorically, or mythologically, the referential meaning is the ability of the word or statement to bring to mind an aspect of its referent within a context. To speak of language as literal in the absolute sense, that is, that the words are absolutely identical to that to which they refer is simply wrong-headed. To say that a language is absolutely relative also misses the point. The community which develops a language and gives it referential significance does so from a given perspective. Language is subject to time, place, and the skills which are transmitted through the community which develops the language through its usage. It is for this reason necessary for a reader of the language to share in the paradigms which have been used in the formation of communication. The language of the Bible can not be fully understood until one is willing to accept the context and the paradigms of the people who produced it and have used it.

The study of any religious text be it Hindu, Buddhist, Confucian, or Christian requires that the reader of the texts of that religion get into the linguistic practices of the community which professes the religion. To look from the outside and attempt to determine what is going on with the processes of a religious group is to understand that religion without the necessary behavior that it takes to make sense of their text. In what follows it will be my intention to read the text as one might understand it with the commitments of the community which has given rise to its existence. This is a skill which may or may not have been mastered adequately. All communication requires a fiduciary relationship between the speaker/writer and the hearer/reader. Communication is never perfect, but understanding is more complete if these parameters are met to the best of our ability.

The second type of meaning that we look for in a text is its significance, the weight which a word or statement has or acquires for its reader. The *significance* or meaning of a text is the importance, force, or demands of the text's message on the reader, the value the text has for those whose life style and personal commitments are shaped as a consequence of engagement with the demands of the text.10

The second way in which we read the Bible to discover meaning is different from the first. The second type of meaning we look for the *weight* of the words or statements. The significance or meaning of a text is the importance, force, or demands of its message on the reader, whose lifestyle and personal commitments are shaped as a consequence of engagement with the normative aspects of the text.

The referential meaning of Lincoln's "Gettysburg Address," what the words referred to as Lincoln delivered them has not changed over the years. But the significance, the meaning of the "Gettysburg Address" changed almost immediately from the time it was given to the weeks that followed. It's significance, its importance, its role as part of American history is far greater than it was when it was delivered at Gettysburg. It has become one of those definitive statements about American values.

Some statements are no more than a statement which brings to mind a referent or series of referents. But other statements are important because they carry authoritative weight in a community. This does not mean that they are authoritative in and of themselves, but because the community which uses them agrees that they are of value or weight.

Religious and certain ideological texts have weight, i.e. carry special significance, in the communities in which they are authoritative. Scriptures such as the *Vedas*, the three baskets of Buddhist's text, Confucius' *Five Books*, the *Quran*, and ideological texts like Mao's, *Little Red Book*, and Marx's, *Das Capital*, and Hitler's, *Mein Kampf* have been more or less significant in communities where their usage is one or more of the following ways: constitutive statements, exemplary statements, prescriptive statements, and prioritizing statements. Like the previous distinctions we have made with regard to referential meaning, these distinctions are analytic and often overlap in an actual text.

There are three sources of significance: (1) Significance which is derived from an authority; for example, the pronouncements of a prophet. (2) Significance which rests on *truth* or a process of legitimizing the statement; for example, "All men are created equal." rests on a *truth* recognized and institutionalized by the founding fathers of the United States. (3) Sometimes significance is accorded a statement because it is linked to or supercedes the significance of another accepted weighted statement. For example, "You have heard it said in times past,... but I say to you."

To understand what is being claimed here for significant meaning, let us look at several types of *weighty* statements to see how their significance is more than their ability to represent their references. (1) A constitutive statement is one which, like the American Constitution, is a *foundational* statement or set of statements, which creates and sustains a value system and is necessary to the understanding and practices of the values which it states. It carries the ultimate weight in the judicial process of which it is a necessary part.

It became what it is through a long process of adjudication and legitimization, and can not be ignored by anyone within the judicial structures of the country of which it is constitutional. (2) An exemplary statement, on the other hand, is a *representative* statement that expresses a feature of a value system, but is not a universal foundational principle. These statements are not necessary to a value system, but they are examples of the value system which they reflect. Often in the Scriptures they are expressed through biblical stories which form precedents for future behavior. (3) Statements which have prescriptive significance are those that call on us to act in a specific manner. Constitutive statements have broad prescriptive force, but other statements are more particular and are addressed to specific acts such as commands, injunctions, and direction which one is enjoined to follow. These may be expressed as direct commandments as in the Old Testament law or the New testament Sermon on the Mount. (4) Prioritizing statements are those statements which organize a system of values in terms of importance; they tell us the role in the over all value structure that a given normative statement may have. When it is asked of Jesus, "What is the greatest commandment?" he is being asked a prioritizing question. The first and greatest commandment is "...to love the Lord your god with your whole heart and mind and your neighbor as yourself." Jesus is not only repeating a prescriptive statement, he also is giving it priority over other prescriptions. As a prioritizing statement it gives preeminent weight to a given prescription. It is a normative statement about other norms.

When we are reading Scripture there are times when the priority of a passage changes, its significance is altered within Scripture itself. In Mathew 5:38-42 Jesus says,

> Again you have heard it said, 'An eye for and eye and a tooth for a tooth,' but I say unto you, 'Do not resist one who is evil. But, if anyone strikes you on the right cheek, turn to him the other also, and if anyone would sue you and take your coat, give him your cloak as well, and if any one forces you to go one mile, go with him two miles. Give to him who begs from you and do not refuse him who would borrow from you.'

Jesus reconstitutes the significance of the command, he does not change the referents which the passage had in Exodus 21, but he relegates the initial significance of the precedent to the past. It now carries less weight, significance, or meaning. It has been replaced by a higher righteousness.

The entire Epistle to the Hebrews is a book which gives the Old Testament practices of Israel new significance in the light of Jesus of Nazareth. The referential meaning of the Old Testament practices is not changed, but their significance meaning is reinterpreted by the writer.

In looking at the significance of a particular passage of Scripture the contemporary reader may want to know more than the significance of the story in its immediate Biblical setting. Its significance in the context of the Scriptures as a whole may be somewhat different. The reader also may want to know the diachronic significance which the passage has had in the life of the Biblical community and the Church, the significance or significances (more than one meaning) which the Church throughout history has given the text. These subsequent claims carry weight according to the action of the Church or a community of worshippers within the larger Church.

When we look for meaning in the Scripture we not only look for information in the text, but also we look for its significance to the user of the texts, to its readers. What is the importance or function of the text in the community which canonizes it as Scripture? What is the process by which a text becomes part of accepted Scripture? What has its significance been in the history of God's people?

The significance of a text is not limited to its Biblical contexts or to the history of the Church, it also has contemporary meaning. Many times the meaning of a passage takes on new significance because of the situation of the contemporary reader. The narratives about the deliverance of the Children of Egypt are narratives which often gain new significance when they are read by a new generation of oppressed people. For Martin Luther King Jr. the story of Moses' deliverance of the Children of Israel out of bondage carried a great deal of meaning, significance, because it *spoke* to his current situation The narrative about the exodus forms for the religious reader a precedent on which a reader can act now.

An historical critical scholar may look for the original referential meaning of the text. The modern reader who is searching for personal relevance of the text and the minister who is interpreting the text for a congregation not only looks for the original referential meaning, but its current significance as well.

When the Gospel writers made the claim that Jesus was the Christ, this was not just a piece of information which was obvious to those who observed Jesus of Nazareth. This was a constitutive claim for his significance. When the early church proclaimed Jesus Messiah was Lord, it was not just a factual statement which they were making; it was a constitutive claim to his significance, his meaning for human spiritual life. When a contemporary Christian reader reads these claims, they are claims which address him now, not just claims which are addressed to the people of Jesus' time or past readers.

For the Church and the religious reader, the Bible is significant information about the past which provides a program for the present as well. It is a set of constitutive, exemplary, directive, and prioritizing claims. It is a set of statements claimed by the community of faith to have universal and continuous relevance, significance in understanding God, ourselves, and what we should morally and spiritually do. Its significances determine our values and norms. We read the information which is there because it has defining importance, significance, to us now.

Both the Academy and the Church may be interested in the value which the text had to its original audience or audiences; however, the Bible is not "Scripture" or the "Word of God" for the Academy. Consequently the significance which the text has for its contemporary users in the Church is different than it is in the Academy where the primary issue is simply what was said. For the Church the value of the text -- for those who have treated it through history as authoritative for their understanding of God, themselves, and a code of conduct --is part of its contemporary significance, its meaning. The history of canonization and the value of the text to predecessors within the traditions of the Church are part of its current significance, i.e., meaning, within that tradition. The value, force, and demands of the text throughout the life of the Church are often critical to interpreting the significance a text currently has in the life of the Church.

The third sense of meaning involves the consequences or outcomes of the use of the text for a given community. Humans use language to communicate descriptions, direct actions, to question, to express emotions, etc., for behavioral goals. When we communicate, we act. The actions which we take with language are part of the meaning of our communications. We know we have successfully communicated when there is an appropriate behavior response or consequence to what has been written or stated. We know that what has been stated is meaningful communication by the outcome which occurs as a result of the language that was used.

Sometimes the consequences of certain statements have immediate physical effects. If we talk about the sourness of squeezing a lemon in one's mouth or letting the juice run down our tongue, we often discover that we are salivating just by telling about the experience.[11] There are other times where the effects are both psychological and physical. There is a phenomenon in hospital pastoral care which is called "permission to die." Almost every chaplain who has been around hospitals very long has experienced it. A patient is alive who should be medically dead; the patient clings to life and will not let go in spite of the pain to themselves and to others. It is often the case that person will "let go" and allow themselves to die when they are given verbal permission to do so by their family, minister or doctor. This is not an unusual process; it happens very commonly.

All communication takes place intentionally. We communicate in order to effect, cause, or create some result. The third understanding of meaning is consequential meaning, the result that comes from the use or reading the text. You have heard it said, "Sticks and stones may break my bones, but words will never harm me." This is experientially not true. Sticks and stones may break your bones, and words can hurt like hell. Words do have behavior consequences.[12]

Sometimes the consequences of statements have social significance. If a man and a woman come before a minister or Justice of the Peace with a proper license, and the official says to them "Do you take this woman to be your lawfully wedded wife? Do you take this man to be your lawfully wedded husband?" When both say "I do" and the official says "I now pronounce you man and wife," their status is never the same. Because the license (which is just words) and the ceremony (which is just words) are properly enacted, the two individuals will never be single again. They may be divorced, widowed, separated, but never single again. Their legal, social, family, and personal status along with their responsibilities and expectations in life, have been changed.

If, after a trial (a language event) in which the jury has pronounced you guilty (another language event), the judge says "I now sentence you to twenty years in the State Penitentiary," then those words are going to put you behind bars because they have consequence. That is part of their meaning.

The consequence of Lincoln's signing the Emancipation Proclamation was the end of slavery in the United States. What the Emancipation Proclamation meant and means is not only what it referred or refers to, but what transformational consequences it had and continues to have.

Many times the action to be taken with a text is tied to a given genre -- Scripture includes lamenting, covenanting, and bonding statements. There are commands, warnings, statements of forgiveness, directives, precedents, and judgments, praise, thanksgiving, constitutive passages, blessings and curses, encouragement, promises, predictions, and statements which provide emotional expression, release and transformation, etc. The Academy may be interested in the literary nature and historical usage of these various genre in the text, but it is not particularly concerned with the use which the text may have in the shaping of the life style and behavior of a contemporary Church community.

The user of the Bible as Christian Scripture is interested in the consequential meaning of the text; the consequences of the use of a given text are critical to its meaning. The consequential meaning of a text is often a source of some, if not all, of its significance meaning.

Reading the Bible as Christian Scripture is always an act of searching for discovery. A reader brings to the texts as much relevant knowledge as he has acquired in order to understand the text. Every bit of training in the process of understanding texts and religions is helpful in the process of discovery. What the readers should not do is to try to make what is said in the text conform to insights that they have been taught that presuppose a different set of normative paradigms about God, the world and themselves. When a reader goes to the Scripture it should be with anticipation of being enlightened by the texts.[13] The same is true for interpreters of the texts. What the interpreters of the text should do is to lead those being instructed in the act of discovery. If the interpreter attempts to redefine what is said in the text to fit some other set of paradigms or world views, then what the text itself says will be inevitably hidden. An interpreter should be a facilitator in reading what the text has to say for itself.

In the life of the Church these three senses of meaning -- referential, significance and consequential -- are inseparable, but the first sense is generally pursued without the second or third. Moreover, when the significance or consequential meaning of a text is purposed, it is usually not for the same goals sought by the interpreter for the current life of the Church. The process of interpreting Scripture for its referential, significant, and consequential meaning in the life of the Church may include the historical and literary concerns, but the Church is guided by the use of Scripture to deepen the commitments and relationships of the Church community. The biblical readers who are interpreting the Scriptures for the life of the Church do not merely discover the content of the message, its value, and its consequential use to its community of origin; their interpretation is an application of the message to a worshipping community that has accepted the text as its current norm and uses it to shape its life style.

In the life of the Church these three senses of meaning, *referential*, *significance* and *consequential* are inseparable and they are for the most part alien to many of us because we think that the only meaning of language is referential. In the coming chapters I want first to deal with what the Scriptures themselves tell us about how the texts became significant in the life of the biblical communities. This will not only describe how the words of prophets and kings were deemed authoritative, but it will also deal with how the record of events and the words of prophets and witnesses became established.

Greek culture, beginning with Parmenides, developed concepts of truth and falsity which were underwritten by reason. However, biblical narratives, prophetic statements, and other texts became authoritative through other processes. In the following chapter we shall deal with the words of prophets, the practice of Israel's kings, and the function of witnesses and signs.

There are four theories of truth in Western Philosophy: the correspondence theory, the coherence theory, the pragmatic theory and (less universally accepted) the existential theory. The correspondence theory states that a statement is true if it corresponds to reality, however the term reality may be defined. In the Western world this is our "common sense" understanding of "truth." A fact is one which corresponds to what we consider to be "reality." This theory inevitably rests on one's metaphysics and what is deemed to be real. Parmenides thought that sense data was not reliable because our senses were not capable of seeing genuine reality; therefore, he proposed that truth referred only to that reality which one arrived at dialectically. Plato, Aristotle, and the Stoics further developed this thesis into formal systems of logic. The Coherence theory of truth developed with Descartes and the Rationalist philosophers of the Enlightenment. It has been developed into symbolic logic and various forms of theories having to do with the logical coherence of concepts. Pragmatic truth is a theory developed primarily in the twentieth century to deal with experimental truths. One states a hypothesis, experiments with that hypothesis, and discovers the truth when the results of the experimentation confirm the conclusion which the hypothesis anticipated. Existential truth is a form of immediate verification of subjective claims through the process of undergoing them.

In the following chapter we shall deal with the words of prophets, the practice of Israel's kings, and the function of witnesses and signs. Biblical scholars have for the most part ignored the manner in which the biblical writers authenticated their messages. We have bought into the common sense idea that a statement is true if it corresponds with reality. This sets up the problem between biblical paradigms and scientific paradigms. The biblical writers did not do the kind of metaphysics that would lend itself to the correspondence theory. When contemporary scholars try to authenticate a biblical statement, they rely on the common sense understanding of reality which is part of our scientific paradigms.[14] Biblical statements cannot be verified in the normal scientific manner because the reality which lies behind the biblical worldview does not correspond to that which can be either empirically verified or is logically necessary.

The argument which I want to make in the next chapter is that statements in the Bible are *established*, which is to say they are considered to be the case if they can be authenticated by a prophet, in some cases by a king, by signs and wonders, or by witnesses. I accept that what is *established* in the mouth of two or more witnesses in biblical writings is a matter of fact. Most of the biblical writers did not have access to dialectic concepts of truth, nor does it appear in the text that they had a single epistemology which they taught as a normative source of revelation or canonization. What they did have they have recorded in the Scriptures, to which we will turn in order to understand what they considered to be matters of fact.[15]

 END NOTES

---

[1] E.A. Nida, Toward a Science of Translating With Special Reference to Principles and Procedures Involving Bible Translation, Leiden, E.J. Brill, 1964: E.A. Nida and C.R. Taber, The Theory and Practice of Translation, Leiden, E.J. Brill, 1969; J. De Waard and E.A, Nida, From One Language to Another, Nashville, Thomas Nelson, 1986; Stanley E. Porter and Richard Hess (eds.) Translating the bible: Problems and Prospects, Sheffield, Sheffield Academic Press, 1999.

[2] C.K. Ogden and I.A. Richards, The Meaning of Meaning ,New York, Harcourt, Brace and World, 5th edition 1938.

[3] Paul Ricouer, The Rules of Metaphor, Toronto, 1975, Max Black, Models and Metaphors , Ithaca, N.Y., Cornell University Press, 1962: Sally McFague, Metaphorical Theology, Philadelphia Fortress Press. 1982: James H. Ware, "Metaphor, Use, And Theological Language," Paper given at the Society for Philosophy of Religion, Athens, GA, 1985.

[4] The manner in which we learn the use of language engages us not only at the conscious level, but at the neurological and physical level also. The process of communicating with a language is conditioned by our neurological programming. I do not think for a minute that language learning and usage can be reduced to physical phenomena, nevertheless, part of the process of language usage and the process of referring can be the object of physiological inquiry, i.e. language and its usage are part of the physical world in which we live: they are part of our "world," not just our "worldview". Although our thoughts which use language are private, the process of learning a language and communicating with it are not limited to obscure, private, mental processes. Charles Morris, Signs, Language, and Behavior, New York, George Braziller, 1946; Paul Watzlawick , The Pragmatics of Human Communication, New York , 1976.

[5] Bertrand Russell, "Descriptions" in Robert Ammerman (ed) Classics of Analytical Philosophy, New York, McGraw-Hill, 1965,Pp. 15-24, Russell, "On Denoting" in Thomas Olshewsky, Problems in the Philosophy of Language, New York, Holt Rinehart Winston, 1969, Pp 300-311; F.F. Strawson, "On Referring" in Ammerman (ed) Classics of Analytical Philosophy, New York, 1965, Pp 315-335; Peter Thomas Geach, Reference and Generality, Ithaca, N.Y.

, Cornel University Press, Emended Edition, 1962; Willard Van Orman Quine, Words & Objects, Cambridge, Mass. M.I.T. Press, 1960.

[6] Martin Heidegger, Being and Time, New York. SCM Press, 1962; Jacques Derrida, Writing and Difference, Chicago, University of Chicago, 1978.

[7] Michael Polanyi, Personal Knowledge, Chicago, University of Chicago, 1958.

[8] Philip Jenkins, The New Faces of Christianity:Believing the bible in the Global South, Oxford, Oxford University Press, 2006.

[9] H. Richard Niebuhr, Christ and Culture, New York, Harper and Row, 1951.

[10] Interpreters of the Scriptures, who think of themselves as objective scientific critics, have been criticized for their lack of personal engagement with a text and for their lack of passion in the hermeneutic process. This is no more clearly stated than in the works of autobiographical and social location reader response advocates. What these "objective" critics often do not acknowledge, or possibly do not understand, is that the term *meaning* means significance rather than referential meaning to them. Most historical critical interpreters are interested in referential meaning and dismiss significant meaning as subjective and relative; and, therefore misleading. See Nancy Miller, Getting Personal: Feminist Occasions and Other Autobiographical Acts, New York, Rutledge, 1993; Dian P. Freeman, Olivia Frey, and Francis Murphy Zauhar (eds.) The Intimate Critique: Autobiographical Literary Criticism, Durham, Duke University Press, 1993; H Aram Vesser (ed.), Confessions of the Critics, New York, Rutledge; Jeffery L Standly, Reading with a Passion, New York, Continuums, 1995; Janis Caple Anderson and Jeffery L Stanley, Taking it Personally, Atlanta, Scholars Press, 1995; Ingrid Rosa Kizberger (ed.), The Personal voice in Biblical Interpretation, London Routledge, 1999.

[11] J.L. Austin, How to Do Things With Words, Oxford, Oxford University Press, 1962; John Searl, Speech Acts, Cambridge, 1969.

[12] Charles Morris, Signs, Language, and Behavior, New York, 1946; Paul Watzlawick, The Pragmatics of Human Communication, New York, 1976

[13] Charles Pierce speaking of himself, states "Endeavoring as a man of that type (experimentalist) naturally would, to formulate what he so approved, he forms the theory that a conception, that is, the rational purport of a word of other expression, lies exclusively in the bearing upon the conduct of life;..."

Charles S. Pierce, "The Experimentalist's View of Assertions" in Yervant H. Krikorian and Abraham Edel, Contemporary Philosophical Problems, New York, Macmillan,1959.

[14] Paul Ricouer rightly points out that, although we accept the fact that our perceptions are shaped by our worldview, nevertheless that which we examine can not be reduced to our perceptions of it; otherwise we fall into the Cartesian trap. Paul Ricouer, "Phenomenology and Hermeneutics," Nous, Vol IX, No. 1, March, 1975.

[15] Jorge J.E. Garcia, How Can We Know What God Means? New York, Palgrave, 2000.

CHAPTER II

Significance:
Truth and Witnesses

Almost every culture and religious tradition has a method to determine the credibility of its traditions. Those elements of the traditions that have been deemed positively credible through some recognized processes that have more significance than those that are simply passed on without examination.

The most familiar process in our modern western societies for validating parts of our traditions are procedures of reason and science and the formal processes of the courts. Although it is fairly easy for most people to recognize that our judicial processes for authorizing statements and claims change over time and are somewhat different from other western countries that share common traditions with us, it is not as easy to accept the fact that the rules of rationality and science change over time.[1] It is difficult for many people to realize that our philosophical and scientific processes are neither eternal nor universally held.

In our judicial system the way a law is authenticated or validated is different from philosophy or science. Laws can be validated by the vote of a legislative body or the decision of a judge or court. In the case of a verdict in a trial, a jury may listen to the presentation of evidence and the testimony of witnesses and come to a conclusion by voting. The process is not governed by strict rules of logic, but by rhetorical arguments and the rules of court procedure. Guilt or innocence is based on the decision of the jury, whether it is justified logically or not. The verdict is authenticated by the judicial process. In our society there are often occasions when two separate judicial processes appear to be in conflict. For example, there probably will be arguments for years to come as to whether O.J. Simpson killed his wife. The jury at his criminal trial said he was not guilty, thereby validating his innocence, whereas the jury in his civil trial determined him to be guilty. Neither jury decision meets the criteria of a wholly rational or scientific process although they meet the requirements of the law and court proceedings. Different processes of validation and authentication within a community and between communities are a basic fact of life that determines the significance of a statement or a conclusion of the certification process.

Sometimes there are hierarchies of validation and certification. In the legal system of the United States if a judge renders an opinion in a lower court, it can be appealed to a higher court until it is either validated or dismissed. The decision may reach the Supreme Court at which point the appeals process ends.

Another form of certification or validation takes place each time someone signs a check; the significance of the validation process can been enhanced by getting the check certified or notarized. The credibility of a statement and its significance rests on the way it is authenticated or established.

In early China the words of an envoy from one prince to another carried significance directly proportionate to the manner in which the envoy spoke. If he spoke eloquently the communication was more significant. This eloquence of style was highly formal and had little to do with argument as we know it. Something similar occurred in the Arabian Peninsula during Mohammed's formation of the Koran. The society used a poetic form of public communication to criticize one another, to praise, and to set forth laws and precedents. These poetic forms carried greater significance if they were done properly. One of the features of Mohammed's authority was the aesthetic quality of his sayings. The aesthetic quality of his use of the genre gave his sayings weight, authority, and significance in addition to the claim that they were delivered to him by the angel Gabriel.

In order to comprehend how the biblical writers understood the process of certifying their claims it is helpful to understand the development of the idea of truth in Western culture. In the early Hellenic culture the words of the poets carried the weight of authority, and one could authenticate a saying or a claim by consulting the poets. Homer, Hesiod, Pindar and the other poets enjoyed tremendous significance as they provided their poetic understanding of the world which later philosophers were to question. The authority of the poets continued for many years after the rise of philosophy. Philosophy introduced a new set of criteria for authenticating statements and giving them overriding significance. With philosophy came the notion of *truth* derived by reasoning. Determining the *truth* of a statement became a primary way of authenticating statements in Western culture.

The formal term *truth* was first brought into Western thought by Parmenides. He used the term *Truth* (with a capital letter) to refer to those statements derived by reason which corresponded to *Reality*, as opposed to those statements which were only opinions that were derived from sense data. The correspondence theory of *Truth,* as it came to be known, assumed a metaphysical Reality beyond experience reality which could only be derived dialectically, i.e., through reason. Metaphysically *Truth* and *Reality* were interchangeable. Linguistically, particular statements which corresponded to that *Truth* stated true opinions. Statements about one's experience derived from observation were never anything but opinions until they had been dialectically processed and all of the flaws of sense data were removed from them.

Socrates and Plato popularized dialectics or reasoning. But it was Aristotle who turned Parmenides correspondence theory on its head. Aristotle held that *truth* was not a metaphysical term, but a term which referred to language itself. Only statements were true or false, never things. A statement was true (1) if it corresponded to the data provided to one's senses by reality (in the common sense meaning of that word) or (2) if a statement were derived logically from other true statements. Aristotle's formulation of the correspondence theory of *truth* is what most people hold as common sense. A statement is true if it replicates reality as we experience it. Literalism, the belief that language replicated reality exactly, is implicit in this understanding of *truth*.

During the Enlightenment the notion of *truth* was directly tied to our acquisition of *ideas*, images and concepts which make up our mental experiences. The meaning of a statement is the way it is perceived. Language names perceptions; it can not create ideas or perceptions without a prior experience of reality. Experiences of our minds are immediate, and experiences of physical reality are made up of ideas or impressions as they occur in the mind.

Commons Sense Realists and some Empiricists continued to insist that our ideas are derived through the senses and correspond directly with reality. Idealists and Phenomenologists, however, deemed those statements to be true which corresponded to the ideas or phenomena which we have in our minds. Both groups held that statements corresponded with ideas, images, impressions or phenomena, all of which could be tested by reason. Implicitly a genuinely true statement could be verified. Language was a conventional set of signs which we learned to associate with given ideas. A statement was true if the ideas to which they were assigned corresponded either with external reality or to experiences in the mind.[2]

Since some mathematical ideas are not derived from the external world but are the product of the mind itself, Descartes introduced a second theory of *truth*, the coherence theory. A statement is true if its signs refer to ideas which hold together logically. Some Phenomenologists and Idealists accepted the coherence theory, because they were skeptical that our ideas of reality actually replicated an external world. When one is limited to experience, there is not a guarantee that an idea replicates reality. The only way to guarantee that an idea is true is that it is logically necessary or coherent with other statements. In the early part of the 20th century the formula which represented the quintessence of Enlightenment thought was: "A statement is true, if and only if, it is logically necessary or empirically verifiable."

Charles Peirce, recognizing the difficulty of knowing "reality," gave us a third criteria, *pragmatic truth*. A statement is true when it is taken as a hypothesis, and experimentation produces the conclusion anticipated by the statement. No explicit claim is made about the relationship of a statement to idea in the mind or correspondence to reality. Statements are "true" and "factual" if their predictive value experimentally works. A good deal of modern science operates with Peirce's understanding of truth. But the methodology is difficult to apply to history, beauty, moral norms, unique events, and experience which are not open to experimentation.

Kierkegaard's understanding of truth as subjectivity was a direct rejection of the previous theories of *truth*. For Kierkegaard one must undergo *truth*. *Truth* is the certitude of immediate experience. *Truth* is encounter. It is not the product of a reflective methodology. It carries its own validation and conviction in the process of existential engagement. A statement is true if it carries with it the immediacy of its own validity. The subjective nature of Kierkegaard's understanding of *truth* prevents its wide support in a culture which expects truth to be objective.

What is common to all these formal uses of the term "*truth*" is that each is a way to authenticate or verify statements. What is stated "is the case" either by correspondence, coherence, pragmatic usage or subjectively. None of these theories treat "*truth*" as a relative matter. As metaphysics, epistemology, and linguistic assumptions have changed, new rules for determining "*truth*" have evolved. There are ample grounds to acknowledge other formal ways of authenticating statements and other theories of "*truth*" which can be used to determine "what is the case" without falling into relativism.

Some churches in our contemporary world have recognized the need for criteria to determine the *truth* or authenticity of what they believe and practice. The Roman Catholic Church has three criteria: (1) the agreement of all Roman Catholics (or in its attenuated form) the universally held position of all Roman Catholic Theologians, or the Magisterium, or the congregation of the church (but not necessarily every person); (2) the proclamation of the bishops meeting in Council; and (3) the Pope's declaration ex cathedra. John Wesley's quadrilateral criterion for Christian doctrine and practice which appears in the United Methodist Discipline gives four broad criteria: (1) Scripture, (2) Tradition, (3) Experience, and (4) Reason.[3]

If persons are to understand the significance or weight of a statement, they must understand that the statement is made within an established set of community standards. Statements, claims, rulings, promises, etc., are stated to meet the criteria of their linguistic community. To try to authenticate or verify (or undermine) their significance with a different set of rules and procedures is anachronistic and will lead to a misinterpretation and misunderstanding of the significance of the statement in question.

---

3. BIBLICAL PROCESSES FOR AUTHENTICATING OR VERIFYING STATEMENTS

When one is interpreting the Scriptures to a contemporary audience in the Church, it is essential in dialoguing with the text that we do not read into the text our contemporary scientific and philosophical methodologies for giving significance to a text. In order to understand the text we must realize that the world in which the writer wrote was quite different from modern culture and criteria for validity and authenticity. The text must be allowed to bear witness to its own validity within its own frames of reference. Within the Bible a "true" statement was one that was *established.* It is this significance that is then communicated to the interpreter's audience in a manner which preserves the significance of the text. As was pointed out earlier, we live in a multiverse when it comes to the number of paradigms we use to explain and validate the different worldviews which are part of our current modes of understanding. Just as we would not expect a Hindu or Buddhist to be constrained by our modern scientific and rational paradigms, we should not expect the writer of the Scriptures to conform to our cultures current standards of validation and authentication.

Once an interpreter has discovered what is established in a biblical text under the criteria which the text itself provides, then there is the task of making it meaningful to a reader or audience which is not familiar with the manner in which the Scriptures assert themselves. This means, in most cases, to learn or teach the world of the writer. It is within the whole that there is full appreciation of the writer, not in some isolated passage.

As we shall see, sometime the significance of a given text changes in a different context or in the larger context of the Scriptures as a whole. This is why continuous dialogue with a particular text and the Scriptures as a whole is necessary. The writers of the Scriptures employed at least three different criteria to *establish* the credibility of certain types of statements.

The first of these criteria for establishing a statement dealt with the words of prophets. The question raised was whether a prophet's words were God's words placed in the mouth of the prophet to be delivered to Israel or whether the prophet spoke presumptuously. The criteria are stated in the following context:

> The Lord Your God will raise up for you a prophet like me from
> among you, from your brethren- - him you shall heed – just as you
> desired of the Lord your God at Horeb on the day of the assembly,
> when you said, "Let me hear again the voice of the Lord my God,
> or see this great fire any more, lest I die." And the Lord said to me,
> "They have rightly said all that they have spoken. I will raise up for
> them a prophet like you from among their brethren; and I will put
> my words in his mouth, and he shall speak my name. I myself will
> require it of him. But the prophet who presumes to speak a word in
> my name, which I have not commanded him to speak, or who speaks
> in the name of other gods, that same prophet shall die."
>
> And if you say in your hearts, "How may we know the words which
> the Lord has not spoken?" When a prophet speaks in the name
> of the Lord, if the word does not come to pass or come true, that
> is a word which the Lord has not spoken; the prophet has spoken
> presumptuously, you need not be afraid of him (Deut. 18: 15-22).

In this passage the reader is not only told what the significance of a prophet's words are, they are the words of the Lord which are to be obeyed, but also how to validate the prophet's words if questions arise. This specific validation process incorporates the importance of the consequences of the prophet's words to the meaning of his statements. Not only does the passage state the significance of a prophet's words, but it also tells how that significance is to be validated or established and thereby given further significance. When a prophet spoke the Word of the Lord, he was not merely predicting the future. God's word created the future that would come to pass. God's word is verified by its power to create that which is its content.

The use of this type of validation or authenticating method not only covers the words of the prophets, but it is cited in the New Testament as well. In Acts 5:27-29 when the Apostles are brought before the High Priest and refuse to accept his order not to teach in Christ's name, an uproar occurred in which Gamaliel, "a teacher of the law," calls on the assembly to recognize that what is not of God fails as the teachings of a certain Theudus and Judas the Galilean had recently done. Gamaliel states of Peter and the Apostles:

> So in the present case I tell you, keep away from these men and let them alone; for if this plan or this undertaking is of men, it will fail, but if of God, you will not be able to overthrow them. You might even be found opposing God (Acts 5: 36-39).

Elijah's confrontation with the priests of Baal on Mount Carmel is an example in the Old Testament text of God is validating His prophet's word over that of the prophets of Baal. In the contest the prophets of Baal are unable to get their god to come down and consume their sacrifice regardless of how they pleaded and mutilated themselves. Elijah, on the contrary, makes it difficult for his sacrifice to be consumed; nevertheless God validates Elijah by consuming his sacrifice (I Kg.18:20-40).

This example of Elijah is actually a crossover between two processes of validation: (1) the words of a prophet are fulfilled, and (2) a sign which exceeds the ability of humans to give takes place. The giving of a sign to validate a statement, a covenant, or an event goes back to the mark put on Cain to keep people from killing him (Gen.4:15). The giving of the rainbow is a sign to validate God's covenant with every living thing not to destroy the world again by flood (Gen. 9:8-17). Some of the tenuousness of signs as validating a message from God is recorded in the story of Gideon, who asks from God a sign. Gideon lays out a piece of fleece and asks that it be wet with dew the next morning and all around it be dry ground if God approved of his attack on the Midianites. The first night the fleece was soaked so that they wrung out an entire bowl of water. However, Gideon is not satisfied with this one time event and requests that the next night the fleece would be dry and the ground around it wet; and, so it happened (6:36-39). Gideon proceeds on the basis of the signs from God. The function of some signs was elliptical, i.e., they validated what was to come and were validated themselves when those events occurred. The signs of the fleece were validated through Gideon's victory. Although signs were not always accepted, they nevertheless played a part in the verification and validation of promises and events.

In the New Testament Jesus performs numerous signs with his healing, the feeding of the five thousand, etc., but these signs were either not recognized as signs or they were often simply treated as magic. Even the signs of the darkening sky and the graves opening at his death did not seem to carry as much weight later on as the words spoken by the prophets and the witness of the disciples. This may be the reason that Jesus gives only an enigmatic sign: when he is tested by the Pharisees who ask him for a sign, he says:

> When it is evening you say, it will be fair weather, for the sky is red and in the morning, it will be stormy today, for the sky is red and threatening. You know how to interpret the appearance of the sky, but you cannot interpret the signs of the time. An evil and adulterous generation seeks for a sign, but no sign shall be given to it except the sign of Jonah (Matt 16:2-4).

The greatest sign, as far as Christians are concerned, is the resurrection. But the event itself remained in question. It was the witness of the disciples and followers of Jesus which was the strongest argument for the resurrection. (We will treat the validation of witnesses later on.)

The citation of the Old Testament prophets by the New Testament writers had a dual effect. On the one hand, in the Jewish community of the Early Church it was already established that the Old Testament prophets spoke the Word of the Lord. To cite the Old Testament prophets was to cite authoritative texts as witnesses to Jesus as Messiah and the Early Church as the Messianic community. But the second effect which the citations of the prophets had was to further authenticate the prophets themselves, because what they had said had come about. From the point of view of the New Testament writers the Old Testament prophets gained significance when their words were seen to be realized in the life of Jesus Messiah and the experience of the presence of the Holy Spirit in the life of the Early Church. Once the prophets were cited to validate Jesus as the Messiah and the Early Church as the Messianic community, the significance of the Old Testament text was raised to a new level in the Church. Once the words of the prophets were cited to underwrite the events of Jesus as the Messiah life, the Old Testament texts significance was greatly enhanced in the new community. The process of validation became elliptical with each text authenticating the other.

The process of verification in Israel was not the same as it was in Greek culture. Verification was not a process which followed the rules of formal logic. God's word was not verified by argument based on the Law of Non-contradiction. Proof that the word of the prophet was the Word of God lay in the consequences of what was said. If the words were from God, then the power of those words to bring about the consequences which they stated was the proof of their authenticity and they were established. Signs also were validated by their consequences.

B. ACCOUNTING FOR CLAIMS AND COUNTER CLAIMS

The second criteria for establishing that a statement was in fact valid or authentic was an adjudication process by the Levitical priests, kings, divinely appointed adjudicators, and/or a church. This form of authentication existed for the establishment of a valid legal opinion. If there are difficulties in interpreting a statute, then the case should be taken to the Levites and judges who are in office at the time.

> If a case arises requiring decision between one kind of homicide and another, one kind of legal right and another, or one kind of assault and another, any case within your towns which is too difficult for you, then you shall arise and go to the place which the Lord your God will choose, and coming to the levitical priest, and the judge who is in office in those days, you shall consult them, and they shall declare unto you the decision (Deut. 17:8-9).

It is quite clear that the content of statues which Israel had were not always clear as to their meaning and application in every subsequent situation.

How the law was to be subsequently interpreted was actually written into the law itself. There had to be a way in which a "true" interpretation of the law could be adjudicated. Within the law itself these interpretations were given absolute authority in their adjudication:

> Then you shall do according to what they declare to you from the place which the Lord will choose; and you shall be careful to do according to all that they direct you: according to the instructions which they give you and according to the decision which they pronounce to you, you shall do; you shall not turn aside from the verdict which they declare to you, either to the right hand or to the left. The man who acts presumptuously, by not obeying the priest who stands to minister there before the Lord your God, or the judge, that man shall die; so you shall purge evil from Israel. And all the people shall hear, and fear, and not act presumptuously again (Deut. 17:10-13).

In the Deuteronomic tradition it appears that this adjudicatory function was passed on later to the kings of Israel, who are enjoined in the law to make a book for themselves from the established statutes which had been the charge of the Levitical priests. (Deut. 17:14-20)

> And when he sits on the throne of his kingdom, he shall write for himself a book a copy of this law, from that which is in charge of the Levitical priests: and it shall be with him, and he shall read in it all the days of his life, that he may learn to fear the Lord his God, by keeping all the words of the law and these statutes, and doing them; that his heart may not be lifted up above the brethren, and that he may not turn aside from the commandments, either to the right hand of to the left…. (Deut. 17:18-20a)

It is clear, at least in these passages, that the declarations of the Levites and judges concerning specific cases composed the law and statutes which are *established* as precedents for the kings. These declarations constitute the foundation of Israel's judicial system. There are no appeals here to dialectical justification, to universal principles, or Natural Law. The book which the king is to draw up is of particular cases, claims and passed judicial pronouncements. It was a book of precedents. It is not based on what can be discovered to be universally true about human nature or society. Nevertheless it is constitutive of Israel's judicial system and the king's character and actions.

This book which the king was to compile was to be read by the king that he might fear the Lord, keep all the statutes and laws and remain humble. In I Chronicles 23:24-32 the adjudication of the law is not listed among the tasks of the Levites under David. However, in II Chronicles 19: 8-11 Jehoshaphat reappoints the Levitical priests as judges. With the demise of the kingship the adjudication of the law seems to have passed over into the prophetic voices and eventually revert to the Levitical priesthood (Ezekiel 44:24). There does not seem to be any Biblical textual authority for the process of adjudicating the law to be put out into the hands of the Sanhedrin, but it seems to have been done so during the Roman rule until the fall of Jerusalem. Eventually within the Jewish community the process of adjudication passed over into the rabbinical schools.

In the New Testament the authority to adjudicate claims and counter claims passed over to the churches.

> If your brother sin against you, go and tell him his fault, between
> you and him alone. If he listens to you, you have gained a brother.
> But if he does not listen, take one or two others along with you that
> every word may be confirmed by the evidence of two witnesses. If
> he refuses to listen to them, tell it to the church; and if he refuses
> to listen even to the church, let him be to you as a Gentile and a tax
> collector (Matt. 18: 15-17).

Mathew's gospel has Jesus saying of the Church: "Truly I say to you 'Whatever you bind on earth shall be bound in heaven, and whatever you loose on earth shall be loosed in heaven' (Matt. 18:18). A ruling concerning claims and counter claims from the body of the Church was to be binding.

This second form of establishing statements does not deal directly with the truth and falsity of statements, but with the significance and establishment of certain types of statements. Israel was not without criteria to determine the authority, veracity, validity or authenticity of statements. It was presupposed that if statements were *established* that they had met all the criteria of credibility. It is necessary to appreciate this fact when one is reading or interpreting this material, although the criteria may not be those with which we choose to operate with in our contemporary culture.

WITNESSES

The third criterion deals with what counts as true evidence. A claim or an accusation is established in the mouth of two or more witnesses. Again the authentication of a statement does not depend upon philosophical argument, but it rests on a practice similar to our legal system, i.e., on the corroboration of two or more witnesses.

> A single witness shall not prevail against a man for any crime or for any wrong in connection with any offense that he has committed; only on the evidence of two witnesses, or three witnesses, shall a charge be sustained. If a malicious witness rises against any man to accuse him of wrong doing, then both parties to the dispute shall appear before the Lord, before the priest and judges who are in office in those days; the judge shall inquire diligently, and if the witness is a false witness and has accused his brother falsely, then you shall do to him as he has meant to do to his brother; so you shall purge the evil from the midst of you. And the rest shall hear, and fear, and shall never again commit any such evil among you. Your eye shall not pity; it shall be life for life, eye for eye, tooth for tooth, hand for hand, and foot for foot. (Deut.19:15-21)

The passage not only elaborates the commandment not to bear false witness (Ex. 20:16, Deut. 5:20, Ex 23:1-3) it provides a way for the judicial process to validate the testimony of witnesses. What is important about this process of validating a witness's statement is that it rests in the corroboration of a second witness and the examination of the witness.

It should be recognized that even in ancient Israel the testimony of a witness was not beyond cross-examination and critical scrutiny. Testimony relied fundamentally on the character of those bearing witness, but if there was some doubt concerning the testimony, the parties involved were to be cross-examined by the authority who was judging the matter. Testimony was not considered to be an emotional appeal or an irrational one. The testimony of two or more people who had been critically questioned provided sufficient evidence of a given fact to establish it.

The claim of a single witness did not carry the same significance. In Deuteronomy we are told that a man could be put to death on the testimony of two witnesses, but could not be put to death on the word of one witness (Deut. 17:6 ; Ex. 25:30). This process is interesting in both its similarity and difference to our own thinking. We would like to claim that what makes a witness's words meaningful, significant and valid is their correspondence with events as they actually occurred. But in the Deuteronomic tradition the validity of the testimony is based on there being a second witness, not on the intrinsic nature of the statement itself, i.e., on its replication of reality. If the same statement, made by two witnesses was made by one witness, it was not established as the case. The statement was not a fact independent of the number of witnesses. This does not mean that no questions were raised. Questions could be raised with the witnesses by the priests and judges.

The determination of the priest and judges was to be final, and a person who acted presumptuously and disobeyed the verdict which a priest or judge gave was subject to the death penalty (Deut.17:8-13). The final appeal of the Deuteronomic passage is not to an abstract notion of the truth or falsity of statements, but primarily to the testimony of witnesses and secondarily to the deliberation of the proper authorities. The significance of a statement did not rest solely on its content, but on how many witnesses attested to it and what authoritative person validated it.

In Israel the process of validating an accusation in the mouth of two witnesses was not always used honorably. When Naboth refused to sell his vineyard to Ahab, Jezebel wrote a letter under Ahab's signature to the nobles and elders of Jezreel that they should get "two base fellows" to accuse Naboth of cursing God and the king. The two bore false witness against Naboth and he was killed, leaving the vineyard for Ahab's taking (I Kg. 21:24). The fact that the practice was abused did not prevent its being the grounds for authenticating, validating, and establishing claims, accusations, and false statements in Israel.

In the New Testament we also find a narrative in which the witness process was subverted. In Acts 6:8-7:60 a group of men were bested in a dispute with Stephen, and the text says:

> Then they secretly instigated men, who said, "We have heard him speak blasphemous word against Moses and God." And they stirred up the people and the leaders and the scribes, and they came upon him and seized him and brought him before the council, and set up false witnesses who said, "This man never ceases to speak words against this holy place and the law; for we have heard him say that this Jesus of Nazareth will destroy this place, and will change the customs which Moses delivered to us." (Acts 6:11-14)

When at the end of Steven's sermon they cast him outside the city to be stoned, according to the law, it was the task of those who witnessed against him to be the first to carry out the sentence (Deut.17:7). And, we read: "...the witnesses laid down their garments at the feet of a young man name Saul,"(Acts 7:58).[4] This particular story shows that the laws concerning witnesses and the processes which were dictated in Deuteronomy were still in effect in Jewish culture at the time of Christ.

It appears that the use of two or more witnesses to establish the validity of a claim in the New Testament era was not limited to the judicial system, but was broadly used to establish authentic claims of various kinds. These regulations were also followed in the Church. We have already seen above that if a brother trespasses on another, one is first to go to him in private. But, if that fails to bring about a resolution:

> ...then take with you one or two more, that in the mouth of two witnesses every word may be established. And if he shall neglect to hear them, tell it to the Church; but if he neglect to hear the Church let him be unto thee as a heathen man and a publican. (Matt. 18:15-17)

In the Early Church two witnesses were used not only to settle disputes (Matt. 18:18), but to effect the results of prayer and to affirm God's presence (Matt. 18: !9-29). The use of witnesses to validate statements and claims was a powerful mechanism for enhancing the significance of what was written or spoken. In the symbolic world of the Scriptures the testimony of two witnesses is evidence which establishes what is stated or claimed as fact. It is implicit in the citation of the witness of the prophets.

The Gospels are replete with examples of the practice of establishing the validity of what is said in the mouth of two or more witnesses. Jesus' trial before Caiaphas as recorded in Matt. 26: 59-68 reflects the process of determining quilt and innocence in the mouth of two witnesses. After having difficulty finding two witnesses who agreed to testify against Jesus, two false witnesses came forward saying, "This fellow said, I am able to destroy the temple of God and build it in three days…." The significance of what these witnesses said is superceded only by what Caiaphas considers Jesus' blasphemy. Caiaphas says, "He has uttered blasphemy. Why do we still need witnesses?" It is in this context that Peter denies his association with Jesus three times, thereby bearing false witness at a very critical time (Matt. 26: 69-75).

It is no accident that Jesus commissions his followers in the Fourth Gospel with the promise of the coming of the Holy Spirit to be his witness (John 15: 26-27). In Acts they are told again after the resurrection to wait for the empowerment of the Holy Spirit and then to be his witnesses in Jerusalem, Judea, Samaria, and to the ends of the earth (Acts 1:8).

Luke begins his gospel with the statement that he is recounting the story of eye witnesses, having followed the matter closely for some time, that Theophilus may know the truth concerning these things which he has been informed (Lk.1:1-4). In Luke when Jesus appoints seventy of his followers to go before him healing and preaching, "The Kingdom of God has come near to you." he sends them two by two (Lk.10:1-12).

The writer of the Gospel of John uses the theme of witness and witnesses throughout the gospel. Almost every episode recorded in the Fourth Gospel is either an account of a witness or a dialogue concerning witnesses to Jesus as the Christ. John the Baptist is sent by God to bear witness to Jesus as the Christ. He is sent by God to bear testimony, to witness, to Jesus (John 1:6-8, 15, 19ff). John also bears witness that Jesus' words and deeds are themselves God's witness in and to Jesus (John 3:22ff, 31-36; see also 10:25ff), The writer has John the Baptist saying of Jesus' testimony:

He bears witness to what he has seen and heard, yet no one receives his testimony; he who receives his testimony set his seal to this, that God is true, for he whom God has sent utters the words of God, for it is not by measure that he gives the Spirit.... (John 3:32-34)

In the Gospel Jesus does not trust himself to human witnesses because he knows that they are unreliable (John 2:23-25, 5:34). Nevertheless, the Gospel writer tells of the impact of the testimony of the Samaritan women coupled with the words of Jesus (John 4:39-40).[5] In the fifth chapter the writer links Jesus' witness to his authority as a judge and to the witness of Moses and the Scriptures (John 5:30-47). When the Pharisees accuse Jesus of bearing witness to himself, which would make his witness false, he counters by quoting the Deuteronomic rule about two witnesses and claims that God is his witness (John 8:13-19). Throughout the Gospel a great deal of attention is paid to the consequences of Jesus' words which are seen to validate what he says, just as the consequences of the words of a prophet validated what the prophet said. In John's Gospel the promise of the abiding presence of the Spirit is associated with God's witness to Jesus and to the authenticity of the disciples' witness (John 16:13-15). The book concludes with the writer claiming to bear witness to what he has written (John 21:24). The significance of the Gospel of John clearly appeals to the Deuteronomic process of validating the words of a prophet, the word witnesses, and the word of judges. Who Jesus is and what he says are not validated by Socratic inquiry or logical argument, they are validated by testimony and witnesses and the communities' accepted rules which govern them.

For Paul in I Corinthians, the fifteenth chapter, the argument for Jesus' resurrection from the dead is based on witnesses to his post-resurrection appearances: Cephas, the twelve, over five hundred, James, all the Apostles and Paul himself. Paul cites the Deuteronomic regulation about accusations to the Corinthians in his second letter to them (II Cor. 13:11).

In the Pastoral Epistles Timothy is instructed that accusations of an elder person should be made only in the mouth of two or three witnesses (I Tim. 5:19).

The same type of authentication process occurs in the second chapter of Hebrews: "It was declared at first by the Lord, and it was attested to us by those who heard him, while God also bore witness by signs and wonders and various miracles and by gifts of the Holy Spirit distributed to his own will" (Hebrew's 2:3b-4). It is echoed again in the eleventh chapter where the writer claims that the faith of the dead witness to the promises of God. After citing the faith of the patriarchs from Abel and Abraham to David, Samuel, and the prophets, the writer says: "Therefore since we are surrounded by so great a cloud of witnesses, let us also lay aside every weight, and sin which clings so closely, and let us run with perseverance the race that is set before us..." (Heb. 12:1).

The weight of the testimony of the patriarchs is a powerful argument within the symbolic world in which the readers function. The writer already pointed out that those who despise the law of Moses die without mercy under the testimony of two or three witnesses (Heb.10:28).

One of the more forceful, yet somewhat enigmatic appeals to witnesses in the New Testament is in I John. The writer says:

> This is he who came by water and blood, Jesus Christ, not with water only but with water and the blood. And the Spirit is the witness, because the Spirit is the truth. There are three witnesses, the Spirit, the water, and the blood; and these agree. If we receive the testimony of men, the testimony of God is greater; for this is the testimony of God that he has borne witness to his Son. He who believes in the Son of God has the testimony in himself. He who does not believe God made him a liar, because he has not believed in the testimony that God has borne to his Son. And this is the testimony, that God gave us eternal life, and this life is in his Son. He who has the son has life; he who has not the Son of God has not life (I John 5: 6-12).

It is anachronistic for a modern reader to overlook or dismiss the arguments as lacking force because we are accustomed to other forms of argument and validation. It appears that within the community of Scripture users that the function of witnesses to validate statements and claims was a powerful mechanism for enhancing the significance of what was written and spoken. It is no wonder that one of the Ten Commandments is not to bear false witness. Witnessing was at the very foundation of establishing that which was in fact the case. The recognition of the force of the testimony of witnesses is essential to the understanding of the force of many statements in Scripture and should be recognized as one reads the texts in the Christian community. In the symbolic world of Scripture, testimony is reasonable evidence which establishes what is stated and claims to be fact.

---

[1] Michael Polanyi, Personal Knowledge, Chicago, University of Chicago Press, 1958.

[2] The Enlightenment notion of the correspondence theory has a tremendous appeal because it appears to represent the way in which we make true statements in everyday life. We take for granted that we accurately describe the objects which we see, hear, touch, taste and smell. The referents for our statements are physical, space-time objects which we not only experience in common, but which can be experienced repeatedly. Because we believe that meaningful words have referents, it is easy to think that whenever we make statements that are meaningful to ourselves and others there must be referents for these statements which are real, objective, in the same manner that objects of sense experience are real, common to us all, and repeatable. It is a very easy move from describing physical, sense-related objects to considering every descriptive statement as a statement about some objective "thing." But the objective status of a referent for present scientifically observable objects is not the same as the objective status of many other meaningful referents. Although it may be the case, i.e., an objective reality, that "John is Henry's friend," friendship is not a physical object, and the statement is not verifiable in the scientific terms. Nor is it possible to treat the significance or importance which an event or object has in the same manner that one treats physical referents, even though they may be the case. The correspondence theory of the Enlightenment was designed for the scientific study of physical objects, and they are incapable of determining the authenticity or validity of statements about relationships, significance, values, beauty, unrepeatable events, or the future. The fact that we claim the reality of these referents does not make them proper subjects of the correspondence theory of the Enlightenment.

[3] Joseph D. Stamey, "Hermeneutics and Authority: Hermeneutics of Authority." Paper presented at the Southwestern Division of the American Academy of

Religion, Dallas, Texas, March 2000.

[4] See also Acts 22:17-20 for Paul's account of the event.

[5] This illustration may not be acceptable to those who question its inclusion in the text.

CHAPTER III

Super-session and Significance

In the Bible when there is a statement addressed to one situation and this statement is reinterpreted by another writer and is given a new meaning in a different context, it is called super-session. If this takes place we say that the significance or meaning of the statement has changed. That is to say, the meaning of the statement in its earlier frame of reference is different from the place it receives in the new situation and usually implies that the later writing of the statement supersedes the earlier or original meaning. This may occur even when the words of the new statement are the same as those of the original statement, because the *significance* of what is said has changed from its earlier writing and earlier context. Generally speaking there are three types of superseding statements. The first type not only changes the context of the statements in question, but also changes the *purpose* or end of what is said. The same words may be used, but the purpose that they served in the initial context is different from the purpose they serve in the second or third context.

The second type of super-session occurs when the first writing of the text is replaced by an event or a statement that makes the first writing no longer important; what was said in the first place is *no longer valid* or *applicable* though it was when it was first written. The third type of super-session occurs when a statement is *fulfilled or completed*, that is, when its meaning and possibilities are filled out and go beyond the initial statement to a higher level or its completion.

An example of the first type of super-session is Paul's use of some of the Abraham narratives in Genesis. In Romans the second through fifth chapters, Paul takes the material of Genesis fifteen through seventeen and gives it a new significance without materially changing the wording of the older reference. In his letter to the Romans Paul makes two arguments. He makes the case for righteousness by faith as opposed to righteousness by the keeping the works of the law; and he makes the case that the descendants of Abraham include the uncircumcised as well as the circumcised. Paul argues that Abraham is the paradigm of righteousness by faith.

> What shall we say about Abraham, our forefather according to the flesh? For, if Abraham was justified by works, he has something to boast about, but not before God. For what does the scripture say? "Abraham believed God, and it was reckoned to him as righteousness." Now to one who works, his wages are not reckoned as a gift but as his due. And to one who does not work but trusts him who justifies the ungodly, his faith is reckoned as righteousness (Rom.4:1-5).

Paul points out that Abraham is reckoned righteous before God simply because he believed God.

> In hope he believed against hope, that he should become the father of many nations; as he had been told, "So shall your descendants be." He did not weaken in faith when he considered his own body, which was as good as dead because he was about a hundred years old, or when he considered the barrenness of Sarah's womb. No distrust made him waver concerning the promise of God, but he grew strong in his faith as he gave glory to God, fully convinced that God was able to do what he promised. That is why faith was "reckoned to him as righteousness." But the words, it was reckoned to him, were written not for his sake alone but for ours also. It will be reckoned to us who believe in him that raised the dead Jesus our Lord, who was put to death for our transgression and raised for our justification (Rom.4:18-25).

He is saying that since Abraham is the paradigm for faith, we too are justified by faith, though our peace with God comes through our Lord Jesus Christ. The Genesis narrative is part of the account of how God used Abraham to form his chosen people. It is part of the narrative about the patriarchs of Israel and the formation of God's people. It is in no respect annulled or changed in its place in the Old Testament texts and remains a critical part of the story of God's dealing with Abraham. Paul's use of the text to prove his point about righteousness through faith in no way removes the texts from their original meaning and context.

His case for Abraham being the father of the uncircumcised as well as the circumcised rests on Abraham's righteousness by faith. At the beginning of chapter fifteen in Genesis God comes to Abraham in a vision and promises him that his reward will make him great. But Abraham protests that he is childless. God takes him outside and tells him to look at the heavens and number the stars, and says to him, "So shall your descendants be." Abraham believes the Lord, and it is reckoned to him as righteousness.

God first promised him the land when he was seventy-five (Gen.12:1-4). God further promises him the land between the river of Egypt to the Euphrates (Gen.15: 18), before Hagar bares Abraham Ishmael when Abraham is eighty-six (Gen. 16:15).

When Abraham was ninety nine God appears to him again and makes a similar promise (Gen. 17:1-8). This time God makes his covenant with Abraham that he will be the father of a multitude of nations and adds to it a sign, the circumcision of all males on the eighth day after their birth. (Gen 17:9-27). Circumcision is to be a sign in their flesh of God's covenant with them. In the Genesis accounts God's covenant is clearly with Abraham's physical descendants, whereas Paul makes the point that the promise is to those who are descendants of Abraham by the fact that they believe God in faith and therefore Gentiles are included (Rom.2: 25-3:9). Paul argues:

Is this blessing pronounced only upon the circumcised, or also upon the uncircumcised? We say that faith was reckoned to Abraham as righteousness. How then was it reckoned to him? Was it before or after he had been circumcised? It was not after, but before he was circumcised. He received circumcision as a sign or seal of the righteousness which he had by faith while he was still uncircumcised. The purpose was to make him the father of all who believed without being circumcised and thus have righteousness reckoned to them, and likewise the father of the circumcised who were not merely circumcised but also follow the example of the faith which our father Abraham had before he was circumcised (Rom 4:9-12).

In his argument Paul is able to say that the descendants of Abraham that are mentioned in Genesis are not limited to the physical descendants of Abraham, but include all those who respond to God in faith (Rom. 4: 11-12). God's promise to Abraham in Genesis seventeen reads:

'I am God Almighty; walk before me and be blameless. And I will make my covenant between me and you, and will multiply you exceedingly.' Then Abram fell on his face; and God said to him, "Behold, my covenant is with you, and you shall be the father of a multitude of nations. No longer shall your name be Abram, but your name shall be Abraham, for I have made you the father of a multitude of nations. I will make you exceedingly fruitful; and I will make nations of you and kings shall come forth from you. And I will establish my covenant between me and you and your descendants after you throughout their generations for an everlasting covenant, to be God to you and to your descendants after you. And I will give to you and to your descendants after you, the land of Canaan, for an everlasting possession; and I will be their God" (Gen.17: 1a-8).

Circumcision becomes the sign or seal of the righteousness Abraham had by faith while he was still uncircumcised (Rom. 4:11a). Paul makes it a point that God's promise to Abraham depends on faith, because the promise did not rest on the law but on God's grace. It was guaranteed to all of Abraham's descendants, not just those that kept the law, but also to those who shared Abraham's faith. It is for this reason that Abraham is considered the father of all persons of faith. God's covenant was that he would make Abraham the father of many nations (Rom.4:16-18). According to Paul, the righteousness which God reckoned to Abraham for his faith will also be reckoned to those who believe in Him that raised from the dead, Jesus our Lord, who was put to death for our sins and raised for our justification (Rom.4:24b-25).

Paul makes the jump from Abraham's faith in God to those who put their faith in Jesus. The significance of his reinterpretation is to include both Jews and Gentiles in God's new covenant through Christ. This parallelism between Abraham's faith in God and the faith of the believers in Jesus, does not change the nature of the earlier narrative within its own context, but it decidedly gives weight to the faith which circumcised and non-circumcised had in Jesus. The faith which readers now have in Christ is not limited to the circumcised, but it includes all those who believe in Jesus, Jew and gentile alike. The significance of God's promise is considerably broadened in scope to include everyone who believes in Jesus for justification and righteousness. On Paul's part this appears to be a significant reading into the Genesis narratives. Nevertheless, the Church bought this argument as part of its interpretation of the Scriptures. Its validity seems to rest on the principle of analogy. Abraham's faith is an archetype which should be expected to be repeated throughout Scripture, varying only with the person and circumstance which surrounds them.

The super-session of a New Testament text over and Old Testament text by no means sets aside the Old Testament. Without the Old Testament it is impossible to understand the New Testament. The whole New Testament narrative rests on the religious practices and prophetic words of the Old Testament. It is simply wrong to think that the Old Testament belongs to the Jew and the New Testament to the Christians, or that the God of the Old Testament is different from the God of the New Testament. The two works are indispensable for understanding each other. This is not only true about what has been said above, but it is equally true of the second and third form of super-session.

The second form of super-session is best illustrated in the Book of Hebrews. With the second form of super-session previous events and circumstances are useless or annulled; they are replaced by God with a new set of circumstances and promises. Hebrews probably more than any other book in the New Testament details the manner in which God's revelation, earlier covenants, Levitical priesthood, and the religious practices associated with the temple are superceded by Jesus the Christ, the Son of God. Where the old priesthood, sacrifices, and covenants once were interim measures, now that Jesus the Christ is manifest, the new understanding, promises, and forms of worship replace them.

The prophets spoke in many ways in the time past but now Jesus reflects God's glory and has the very stamp of God's nature upon him (Heb. 1a-3a). He has obtained a higher excellence than the angels (Heb.1:4) and all things are placed under him, although we do not see it entirely at the present (Heb.2:8). Jesus becomes "the merciful and faithful high priest in the service of God, to make expiation for the sins of the people" (Heb.2:17). Jesus is the apostle and high priest of our confession, and is more worthy than Moses, as the builder of a house has more honor than the house. (Heb.3:1-4). Moses was faithful as a servant, but Christ was faithful over God's house as a son (Heb, 3:5-6). The followers of Jesus are now God's house if they hold fast their confidence and pride in their hope (Heb.3:6). Jesus is the new high priest who can sympathize without weakness; because of this, he could offer a sacrifice for not only his own sins but ours as well. He is called to do this even as Aaron was called by God (Heb.5: 1-5). God appointed Jesus as a high priest after the order of Melchizedek (Heb. 5:6). Of Melchizedek the writer says: "He is without father or mother or genealogy, and has neither beginning of days nor end of life, but resembles the Son of God he continues a priest for ever" (Heb. 7:3). And Jesus being perfect as a Son through his suffering became the eternal source of salvation for all those who obey him (Heb.5: 7-9). The writer of Hebrews is rather forceful about repentance:

> For it is impossible to restore again to repentance those who have once been enlightened, who have tasted the heavenly gift, and have become partakers of the Holy Spirit, and have tasted the goodness of the word of God and the power of the age to come, if they then commit apostasy, since they crucify the Son of God on their own account and hold him up to contempt (Heb.6:4-6).

Perfection could not be achieved under the Levitical priesthood. With Jesus the law that the high priest should be of the tribe Levi is replaced by a priest from the tribe of Judah (Heb.7:14) who like Melchizedeck has an indestructible life (Heb.7:15-16). To make sure that his super-session is complete the writer of Hebrew adds:

> On the one hand, a former commandment is set aside because its weakness and uselessness (for the law made nothing perfect); on the other hand, a better hope is introduced, through which we draw near to God (Heb. 7:18-19).

In the past priests had taken their office without an oath, but the writer declares that the Lord has sworn and will not change his mind; "Thou art a priest forever" makes Jesus the surety of a better covenant (Heb.7:21-22). In previous times there were numbers of priests who were prevented by death from continuing in office; but Jesus' priesthood was permanent. His offering was once for all when he offered himself up (Heb 7: 23-25).

Jesus serves before God in a heavenly tent, not an earthly one as in the old covenant. God has made a new covenant in which he will place his laws in their hearts and minds. This new covenant replaces the old covenant which is now obsolete (Heb. 8:15). All of the regulations and equipment of the holy tent of the old covenant are obsolete. Christ serves in a greater, more perfect tent into which he enters one time, not with the blood of animals but with his own blood, thereby securing eternal redemption. (Heb.9:1-14). As the blood of animals was sprinkled over all the instruments of worship, and Moses said that the blood was the blood of the covenant and it purified everything used in worship, so Christ entered the heavenly Holy Place and once for all sacrificed himself (Heb 9:23-28). Under the old covenant and law the process must be performed yearly, now with Christ's sacrifice it is once for all (Heb. 10:1-39).

Essentially the rest of the book of Hebrews is an exhortation to the readers to keep their faith. The writer cites many of the heroes of the Old Testament who kept their faith though all sorts of trials, yet they never saw the completion of God's promise. He encourages his readers to endure divine discipline, continue in brotherly love, and wait faithfully for Jesus the mediator of the new covenant.

The super-session written about in Hebrews makes the Old Testament narratives problematic for the person who thinks that all of the Scriptures are eternally given by God to be obeyed forever in the manner they are given. Hebrews is the best example of how the content of Scripture changes, even to the point of annulling or making earlier statements obsolete. Scripture has continuity, but in that continuity there are changes.

The third type of super-session states the case for a higher form of righteousness than an early form of instruction or law. A given command or law is not rescinded, but it is amended so that it is a higher form of righteousness than the earlier statement. The statement of a higher form of righteousness may be tied to the circumstances in which the older form of the law is stated, it may be pronounced to include more people, or it may address a new issue. Two features of statements of a higher righteousness are always present; (1) The old law or instruction is not done away with but redefined or fulfilled; (2) the higher righteousness is a universal obligation, i.e., it applies to everyone equally.

An example of the third type of super-session is seen in Jesus statement in Matthew five:

> Think not that I have come to abolish the law and the prophets; I have come not to abolish them but to fulfill them. For truly, I say to you, till heaven and earth pass away, not an iota, not a dot, will pass from the law till all is accomplished. Whoever then relaxes one of the least of these commandments and teaches men so, shall be called least in the kingdom of heaven; but he who does them and teaches them shall be great in the kingdom of heaven. For I tell you, unless your righteousness exceeds that of the scribes and Pharisees, you will never enter the kingdom of heaven (Matthew 5: 17-20).

In this statement Jesus makes clear to his listeners that he supports the law, but expects a higher righteousness than the mere fulfillment of the letter of the law as the Pharisees practiced it. He is not only rejecting antinomianism outright, but respects the law of the Old Testament. He says of those who teach people to relax the law they will be called the least in the kingdom of heaven.

The higher righteousness which he is advocating is spelled out in a series of examples. The first is, "You have heard that it was said to the men of old, 'You shall not kill; and whoever kills shall be liable to judgment,'" (Matt. 5:21). Jesus goes beyond the immediate act of killing to the underlying attitudes and actions of the person who would kill another person. One should not be angry with, insult, or curse his brother; these actions that separate persons from one another are so basically wrong in God's sight that one should not bring a gift to the altar until the person has become reconciled with the person with whom he has broken relationships. A person who is accused should even make friends with his accusers. Although the statement is not made in this passage, the higher righteousness involved is to love your neighbor as you love yourself. From this passage to do otherwise is to risk punishment.

Again with the issue of adultery, it is not just wrong to commit the act. Jesus says that the higher righteousness is that one does not look lustfully at women, because that is as much as committing adultery with her in one's heart. Not only is it wrong to break the law, but it is also wrong to say that these statements are hyperbole in order to avoid taking them seriously. To say that if your right eye causes you to sin, it would be better to lose a member of your body than to have your whole body sent to hell. If your right hand causes you to sin, cut it off and throw it away. It is better to lose a part of your body than have your entire self sent to hell. The radical nature of what Jesus is saying cuts through any offhandedness or excuses that the reader might hold. Jesus is not joking; what he is saying is of ultimate seriousness. There is everything to be gained by the higher righteousness, and everything to lose by not following it. There is no cheap grace in Jesus' discussion of a higher righteousness.

The same is true of divorce. Giving a certificate of divorce is not enough for the higher righteousness. In the Mosaic law, if a man wanted to divorce his wife, he was to give a certificate of divorce (Deut.24:1-4). In Mark's gospel when Jesus is asked by the Pharisees whether it is lawful for a man to divorce his wife, Jesus says that because of the hardness of their hearts, Moses gave the ruling that a man must give the woman a certificate of divorce if he is going to divorce her. This ruling was a move toward a higher righteousness because it recognizes that a man has a responsibility to his wife, and this was not always the case in patriarchic societies. Older patriarchic societies did not give a woman any rights. Moses ruling stated that women were not to be treated arbitrarily by their husbands. From the beginning God made humankind male and female, and the two were one flesh. What the gospel of Mark states is that what God has joined together no one should break apart (Mk.10:2-12).

In Matthew's gospel to divorce one's wife for any cause other than the lack of chastity is sinful. It makes the wife an adulteress, when a husband chooses to divorce her for other reasons. Whoever marries a divorced woman commits adultery (Matt. 5:32a). In Mark's gospel Jesus says that whoever divorces his wife and marries another woman commits adultery. The same is true for a woman who divorces her husband and marries someone else (Mark 10:11-12). Unfortunately in the immediate contexts it does not clearly state whether the motive to divorce someone is done in order to marry some one else, or whether or not it is always wrong to marry someone who is divorced regardless of the motive or circumstance.

The reasoning against divorce goes back to God's creation of humankind as male and female, and that marriage makes the two of them indivisibly one. This oneness should not be abrogated. Mark and Luke have very strong language about the marriage of someone who is divorced. For someone to marry after a divorce is to commits adultery (Mk.10: 2-12; Lk. 16:18). The difficulty a reader faces in these passages is that no context is given to determine if there might be a higher righteousness that would permit divorce or remarriage. For example, should a person divorce their spouse because the spouse is seriously abusive to their children? Does Jesus teaching on forgiveness leave room for a divorced person to remarry? In I Cor. 7:10-11 Paul also tells his readers that they should not divorce one another; if they do, the woman should remain single or be reconciled with her husband. A higher form of righteousness is not spelled out, although it would not be difficult to set up some such scenario. Jesus has said more radical things than that men and women are to be considered equally in the case of divorce.

A number of years ago I was asked by a young divorced woman with a four-year- old child whether or not she should remarry. The man she to whom she was married was married previously, and she was not aware of it when she married him; and he was very abusive. That was her reason for divorcing him. Should she go back and remarry the abusive husband to whom she had been married, whom she now knew had been married to someone else? Another man wanted her to marry him. But since she was divorced, wouldn't that make it wrong from them to marry? The only other option was for her not to marry at all and to raise her son without a father figure, which meant in her mind that she had not acted responsibly toward her son. What would be the higher righteousness?

Although Jesus does not say so, the present day Church is left to deal with the issue under the guidance of the Holy Spirit. One can argue, however, from another form of higher righteousness by analogy. In Exodus 20:8-11 the Mosaic Law states:

> Remember the Sabbath day to keep it holy. Six days you shall labor, and do all your work; but the seventh day is a Sabbath to the Lord your God; in it you shall not do any work, you, or your son, or your daughter, your man servant, or your maidservant, or your cattle, or the sojourner who is within your gates; for in six days the Lord made the heavens and the earth, the sea, and all that is within them, and rested the seventh day; therefore the Lord blessed the Sabbath day and hallowed it.

In spite of this law, when Jesus' disciples were walking through a grain field, and picked grain on the Sabbath day to eat, and the Pharisees confronted him about doing something unlawful on the Sabbath. Jesus answered them by pointing out that David entered into God's house and ate the bread of the Presence when he was hungry, which was against the law. Even the priests profaned the Sabbath law and were held guiltless (Matt. 12:1-5).

In the text immediately following this occasion Jesus healed a man with a withered hand on that same Sabbath. When he was challenged, he replied, "What man of you, if he has one sheep and it falls in a pit on the Sabbath day, will not lay hold of it and lift it out?" (Matt. 12: 9-13). And after he has healed the man with the withered hand, he asks: "...is it lawful to do good on the Sabbath?" (Matt. 12: 8, 12) Jesus tells the Pharisees, "For the Son of man is lord of the Sabbath." At the same event as recorded in Mark's gospel, Jesus says, "The Sabbath was made for man, and not man for the Sabbath" (Mk.2:27).

By analogy, with regard to both divorce and marriage to a person who has been divorced, it is consonant with Jesus' teaching that it is possible to redeem any situation which attempts to restore what God has done in creation, and man has destroyed. God did not create males and females joined together for the purpose of conflict or sinning. He created human beings male and female for companionship and reproduction.

However, for the contemporary Church and individual, a higher righteousness can not simply be announced by one person with regard to themselves. What is required in the present day is both the individual and the Church under the guidance of the Holy Spirit agree on a responsible way to act that is a higher righteousness. In the Gospel of John, Jesus tells his disciples that God will send the Counselor, the Holy Spirit, and he will teach you all things and bring to remembrance all that Jesus has taught (John 15:25).

When the Scriptures are either silent or incomplete and interpretations of the material must be made, the Church can always rely on the counsel of the Holy Spirit. The work of the Holy Spirit is always like the work of God himself. It always constrains the person in Christ to act with responsible caring, i.e., love. It always speaks to the Church and the individual in a creative way that reflects the God's creative activity. The guidance of the Holy Spirit is always purposeful, i.e., it points forward to the completion of God's will. It always embodies the holy. Its counsels are both pure and awe inspiring because the Holy Spirit is always God's Spirit which can go beyond human ingenuity.

In deciding the problem whether or not an act is of a higher righteousness, where there is no context to assist the reader, the Holy Spirit guides those who seek his leadership. There always needs to be recognition that something unrighteous has occurred and that it is being redeemed by an act of higher righteousness. A person is dealing with that which is holy. Here the text is basically incomplete with regard to marrying a woman who is divorced. To make her an adulteress if she remarries, makes her a victim the second time. To punish her for a divorce which may or may not have been her fault is less that responsible love. It would seem to me that a higher righteousness would have been an acknowledgement of a sinful act having occurred and a real compassion shown to the woman, particularly if she were not the person initiating the divorce. In Jesus' case the answer he gave was not to attribute blame, but how to please God. To rise to a higher righteousness is to act with the acknowledgement that things are broken, a law has been broken. But action can be taken which supersedes the broken law. Responsible concern under God with the concurrence of the individuals and the Church, approximate the acts of a higher righteousness that Jesus might have performed.

Granted that in our day and time divorce is badly over-used to moderate bad situations; nevertheless, a loving and responsible act of divorce still can recognize that the occasion involves elements of sin, and unrighteousness which need to be set right. One needs to find the most constructive alternative. The same seems to be true with marrying a divorced person. The higher righteousness as it evolves with divorce and remarriage is an example of the continual search with the help of the Holy Spirit for the Church and the individual to do the right thing, i.e., to act under God in responsible love on the part of all the parties, remembering that God did create humankind male and female and made them one in marriage. The higher righteousness may be simply the choice most consistent with what we know about God. Jesus' statements did not abrogate the law; they supersede it.

In Matthew's gospel Jesus continues with his statements which supersede "what had been said of old." It was said, "You shall not swear falsely, but perform to the Lord what you have sworn." Jesus says do not swear at all. "Let what you say be simply 'Yes' or 'No'; anything more than this comes from evil" (Matt. 5:33-37). He continues,

> You have heard that it was said, 'An eye for and eye and a tooth for a tooth.' But I say to you. Do not resist one who is evil. But if any one strikes you on the right cheek, turn to him the other also; and if any one should sue you and take your coat, let him have your cloak as well; and if any one forces you to go one mile, go with him two miles. Give to him who begs from you, and do not refuse him who would borrow from you (Matt.5:38-42). You have heard that it was said, "You shall love your neighbor and hate your enemies." But I say to you, "Love your enemies and pray for those who persecute you, so that you may be sons of your Father who is in heaven; for he makes his sun to rise on the evil and on the good, and sends rain on the just and the unjust. For if you love those who love you, what reward have you? Do not the tax collectors do the same? And if you salute only your brethren, what more are you doing than others? You, therefore, must be perfect; as your heavenly Father is perfect" (Matt. 5:43-48).

These teachings go beyond the normal expectations of both Jesus' society and our own.

These statements of Jesus about the higher righteousness are not open to further interpretation as they stand. In none of these statements is there a third party to be considered. It does not say how your oppressor is oppressing you or oppressing you and your children. There is no ambiguity in what he says. Here the higher righteousness is to be perfect, even as your Father in heaven is perfect. There are no superseding acts of an even higher righteousness. Can these statements become ambiguous when there is a situation which involves others, where some benefit and others are penalized? Certainly! We can interject those ambiguities into the problems, but when we do so as a pretext not to follow them, then we are indeed not acting in good faith. Jesus' form of higher righteousness is not simple or easy.

One of the issues of modern time which was not clearly resolved in the Scriptures is the problem of slavery. It seems to be taken as the normal state of affairs in the text. Paul's letter to Philemon comes very close to superseding the practice of slavery. Paul has found great comfort and encouragement from Philemon, but stops short of commanding him to receive his slave Onesimus back. Onesimus has become like a son to Paul and has served him well. Sending him back to Philemon, Paul says, is like sending my very heart. He would have been more than happy to have Onesimus serve him while he was in prison. He had refrained from sending him because he did not want Philemon to feel compelled to receive Onesimus back. Paul says, "Perhaps this is why he was parted from you for a while, that you might have him back forever," no longer as a slave but more like a brother, especially to Paul, but also to Philemon himself. Paul says to Philemon, "So if you consider me your partner, receive him as you would receive me"(Philemon1:17). If Onesimus owes Philemon anything, charge it off to Paul regardless of what Philemon may owe Paul. Paul says to his friend, "I want some benefit from you in the Lord. Refresh my heart in Christ." He claims that he is confident that Philemon will be obedient and that he will prepare a guest room for Paul, for he hopes to be there as Philemon has prayed. Paul sends his greetings and those of their mutual friends, but he does not ask Philemon to free Onesimus. If Paul represents the Church of his day, it is not free from believing in slavery.

Even though Galatians, which is probably written about the same time states:

> Now before faith came we were confined under the law, kept under restraint until faith should be revealed. So that the law was our custodian until Christ came; and that we might be justified through faith. But now faith has come, we are no longer under a custodian; for in Christ Jesus you are all sons of God, through faith. For as many of you as were baptized into Christ have put on Christ. There is neither Jew nor Greek, there is neither slave nor free, there is neither male nor female; for you are all one in Christ Jesus (Gal: 23-28).

It is in Ephesians that we get a glimpse of how the Church of the late first century thought a slave and a master should behave:

> Slaves, be obedient to those who are your masters, with fear and trembling, in singleness of heart, as to Christ; not in the way of eye-service, as men-pleasers, but as servants of Christ, doing the will of God from the heart, rendering service with a good will as to the Lord and not to men, knowing that whatever good any one does, he will receive the same again from the Lord whether he is slave or free. Masters do the same to them, and forebear threatening, knowing that he who is both their Master and yours is in heaven, and that there is no partiality with him (Eph 6:5-9).

Although the Church has defined the relationship of slave and master as a relationship which takes place under God who is Master of both the slave and the master, it has not found a higher righteousness which delivers both slave and master from the institution of slavery. It will be the nineteenth century before there is a higher righteousness which will do away with the institution of slavery.

Although the Scriptures always assume a society in which slavery is practiced, the early Church went beyond the understanding of slavery of the first century. The relation is mitigated by slaves and masters being united under Christ. The Church is on the way toward a higher righteousness but is not quite able to see it in that day and time. The relationship between slave and master is between two people; at least it is not cast in the form of a social institution which would overlook the behavior of those involved and establish an institutional status quo. We today can see more clearly now that there is almost universal consensus that slavery is wrong. The breaking through to the contemporary scene during the nineteenth century was a terrible struggle with loss of life both in the United States and in other places in the world. For the vast majority of the world slavery as a social institution is seen as sin. Human beings were not created in the image of God to be owned and mastered by other human beings. Freedom from slavery is a higher righteousness for which we can give thanks to God and the work of the Holy Spirit through God's people.

What I am trying to show by the transformation of the laws of our so-cieties to a form of higher righteousness in the modern world, is that God continues to define a higher righteousness as the world changes. We may never reach the time that all laws are superseded by a higher righteousness until the consummation of this age in the Kingdom of God. But there will be effort to define a higher righteousness wherever people try to live their lives beyond what is required by law.

The issue of homosexuality is a case in point. The question has been raised and will not go away until the Church as a whole can come to some form of consensus under the guidance of the Holy Spirit as to what con-stitutes God's will and righteousness. There are two direct references to homosexual behavior in the Old Testament (Lev. 18:22, 20: 13) and at least one in the New Testament (Romans 1: 26-27).

The setting for the first Old Testament passage is related to sexual sins and the worship of Moleck:

> And you shall not lie carnally with your neighbor's wife, and defile yourself with her. You shall not give any of your children to devote them by fire to Molech, and so profane the name of your God: I am the Lord. You shall not lie with a male as with a women; it is an abomination. And you shall not lie with any beast and defile yourself with it, neither shall any women give herself to a beast to lie with it: it is perversion. Do not defile yourselves by any of these things, for by all these the nations I am casting out before you defiled themselves; and the land became defiled, so that I punished its

iniquity, and the land vomited out its inhabitants. But you shall keep my statutes and my ordinances and do none of these abominations, either the native or the stranger who sojourns among you (for all these abominations the men of the land did, who were before you, so that the land became defiled); lest the land vomit you out, when you defile it, as it vomited out the nation that was before you. For whoever shall do any of these abominations, the persons that do them shall be cut off from among their people. So keep my charge never to practice any of these customs which were practiced before you, and never to defile yourselves by them: I am the Lord your God (Lev. 18: 20-30).

It is very difficult to treat these injunctions as unimportant. Homosexuality and bestiality are both part of the same set of injunctions and both are seriously condemned.

The second time that the injunction is made in the Old Testament is in the context of adultery and incest:

If a man commits adultery with the wife of his neighbor, both the adulterer and the adulteress shall be put to death. The man who lies with his father's wife has uncovered his father's nakedness; both of them shall be put to death, their blood is upon them. If a man lies with his daughter-in-law, both of them shall be put to death; they have committed incest, their blood is upon them. If a man lies with a male as with a woman, both of them have committed an abomination; they shall be put to death, their blood is upon them (Lev.20:10-13).

The contemporary debate about homosexuality began with the civil rights movement. Gays and Lesbians claimed the *right* to have sex with others of their own gender. This was a right to use their bodies as they please. This right, they contended, was no different from a woman's right to have an abortion, i.e., to have a right over her own physical being. This right could not be construed as a sin, much less result in the death penalty. Although the argument has passed through many phases that what is com-manded in Leviticus does not apply to a person in the present world; it is superseded. Several arguments have been given for the rectitude of homo-sexuality in the sight of God. Some have said that homosexuality is the way that God created some people; therefore, it is not a sin. Others have given a similar answer that homosexuals are born homosexual; therefore, they can not be condemned for what they are. The moral question now becomes, is this a higher righteousness? Isn't homosexuality an argument for the self- realization of that person? Those who hold the claim that this is indeed a higher righteousness for those who are homosexual and it su-persedes the Biblical injunctions, usually claim that Christians should not condemn homosexuals because the commandment to love one's neighbor is second only to the commandment to love God with one's whole heart, soul, and mind.

The Church is sharply divided over the issue. For the most part theo-logical liberals will support the homosexual's right to his or her sexual preference. However, the majority of the Church, especially in the sec-ond and third world still hold strongly to the belief that homosexuality is wrong.

There seem to me to be two features which are not examined very closely: (1) Not all homosexual acts are acts for self-realization and there-fore a higher righteousness. Even the Greeks, for whom homosexuality was an accepted practice, did not think that all homosexual acts were good. Socrates differentiates in the *Symposium* that some homosexuality appeals to a human's physical pleasures, and does not exist to achieve a higher good. When no distinction is made in the way in which homo-sexual behavior is carried out, there is no guarantee that it will lead to self-realization or to self-indulgence and deprivation.

Even if one agreed that some persons are born homosexual, or even that God has created them as homosexuals, it is not a license to do what-ever one pleases with that predisposition. Some where along the line someone is going to have to define what is good homosexuality and what is bad homosexuality. In most of the current debate the picture painted is two homosexuals bonded to one another's good for life. That is not a very accurate picture of what happens in the real world. One can not avoid the fact that some gays have multiple partners and faithfulness between these partners is not often observed.

(2) The second consideration deals with the commandment to love one

another. To love a person who is gay or lesbian does not turn their deeds into something righteous.

To love some one does not prohibit someone from immoral behavior. Responsible love by someone else does not change the homosexual act. It does change the person who is loving; but it does not keep them from recognizing that homosexual behavior is by no means always the best behavior for those engaged in it. A person can genuinely love a gay or lesbian person without condoning their behavior.

There is one aspect of the issue which is seldom addressed, and that is the penalty for homosexual behavior. I think that it is generally accepted that homosexual not be put to death for homosexual acts. The commandments as written in the text not only make homosexuality wrong, they require that homosexual behavior be punished by death. On this second half of the commandment the Church has reached a consensus as to what is the higher righteousness. Although a person commits acts of homosexuality, they should not suffer the death penalty. This is a super-session of the Old Testament text.

The higher righteousness of homosexual behavior is far from being established. In searching for a higher righteousness the parties engaged in the dispute are going to have to rely more consciously on the work of the Holy Spirit and the nature of Biblical authority. If it is decided that homosexual behavior amounts to a higher righteousness that supersedes the biblical injunctions, it must be universally applied. The nature of a higher righteousness is such that it carries with it a divine mandate to all who believe. For this reason alone I think that it will never be held as a higher righteousness in the life of the Church.

This current analysis of different types of super-session show that what has been written before is often a springboard for a new understanding of biblical material. It is almost always controversial, but in most cases that which supersedes depends upon that which is superseded in order to be understood. One cannot discard that which is superseded without undermining what is said to be superseding. There are not only examples of super-session in the Scriptures, but there are also features of the Scriptures which are going to be superseded, like slavery, by the work of the Holy Spirit in the Church.

CHAPTER IV

Consequential Meaning and The Language of Precedents

The previous chapter sets out the concept of super-session as it applies to the Scriptures and to possible changes in the significance of texts. It also pointed out that new superseding statements and events may still occur in the understanding of the Church under the guidance of the Holy Spirit. In this chapter we will discuss precedents as one form of consequential meaning. Consequential meaning results when language is used to accomplish a particular end, i.e., do something.1 Commands, laws, statutes, demands, orders, instructions, requests, and precedents are all ways in which language is used to get someone to act in a given manner. This chapter will elaborate the place that precedents play as divine injunctions in the Scriptures. Prescriptive statements always have consequential meaning because they require the recipient to do something, to either observe their instructions or to ignore them.

Their very statement demands a response of some sort. Consequences of one type or another, positive or negative, always follow the giving or stating of commands, statutes, laws, demands, orders, injunctions, requests, instructions or precedents.

In the Scriptures there are no philosophical, legal, political justifications, or defenses of God-given prescriptive statements; nor are divine commands justified by reason or based on the laws of nature or metaphysics. God's authority does not need defending. God's instructions and commands do not make up a set of abstractions or universal generalizations as to what God's people should or should not do. They stand on God's righteous will and wisdom.

Divine commands, laws, statutes, instructions, statues, and precedents became established in the biblical community by the work of the Holy Spirit. Through the witness of prophets, kings, priests, prescriptive language was brought into the community and recorded as the Word of God. When this took place God's prescriptive statements became *established in the community both by the acceptance of the community and by the use of the prescriptions in the life of the community.*

In the Scriptures God's commands and instructions often appear in several different genres. There are at least three general types of prescriptive statements drawn up in the Bible. The first is made up of practical instructions. We are accustomed to think of God's instructions as commandments or statutes, but many of God's pronouncements are in terms of the instructions of wisdom. In the wisdom literature we have sayings which carry practical moral weight, but are not actually legal statutes but practical wisdom. The instructions of Wisdom Literature are grounded in life and that which promotes a good life. In the biblical Wisdom Literature, especially Proverbs and Ecclesiastes, God's instructions are based on practical consequences and read like practical advice. But since this type of practical wisdom has its grounding in God's Wisdom, it appears at face value to be good advice. That which is practically wise in the Scriptures carries with it divine approval. It is not like a law or a statute that is given as a categorical imperative, but it carries God's endorsement. It is not a just a statement of divine approval or disapproval; a person who fails to act on God's practical wisdom is guilty of impropriety, because it goes against God's practical wisdom.

The second type of prescriptions given in the Bible is composed of statutes and commandments that make up the formal law codes of the Scriptures. They are almost always stated within a definitive narrative (one that is used to underwrite the nature of the community and its identity, constitutive language) or a prophetic account that gives them a context. In the Bible statutes and commandments are part of Israel's definitive history and are consequently grounded in Israel's life with God.

Divine imperatives, God's commands, statutes, laws, carry more weight than practical wisdom. To disobey them is to sin. God's imperatives are usually given in concrete situations, such as immediately following Israel's exodus from Egypt, or when the Israelites had circled Mount Sinai several years. Divine imperatives are almost always given to the reader of the Bible within a definitive historical context. They are part of the narrative of God's actions and Israel's responses. The bulk of divine imperatives within Israel's history are recorded as part of Israel's wandering through the wilderness. The majority of God's commands in the New Testament are recorded in the Gospels as part of Jesus' life and ministry.

Within the definitive narrative of God and Israel interacting the ordinances and instructions are particular and concrete, and usually are related directly to the events of the full narrative. They describe the prohibited behavior as it would take place in a given setting and for a specific consequence. One such case is clearly stated in the injunction not to wrong or oppress a stranger, because Israelites were once strangers in the land of Egypt (Ex. 23:9). The particular reason for not wronging a stranger is based on the immediately previous condition of the Israelites. The Israelites had been strangers in the Egypt, and they were not to treat strangers in their camp in the way that they were treated in Egypt. The command is not based on a metaphysics or abstract universal principle law, but is given in conjunction with Israel's experience in Egypt that made them a people. The divine instruction about the treatment of a debtor is also spelled out as a concrete case, not as an abstract commandment, because Israelites understood what it meant to be a debtor while they lived among the Egyptians (Ex 22:25-27). They knew what the consequences of being badly treated were, because they had recently suffered those consequences. The stories of the exile were already accepted, established, and now they were used by the Israelites to guide their own behavior.

Most of Israel's early collections of God's commandments according to the texts were given through Moses and make up Israel's criminal code, moral code, and the directions for carrying out Israel's religious life. Genesis, Exodus, Leviticus, Numbers, Deuteronomy, Joshua, and Judges (the last two are an addenda to the first five) set out both the narrative of

God's commands from Adam to the Exodus from Egypt and continue it into Israel's occupation of the promised land. These narratives were Israel's story. God's commandments do not end with the settlement of the land. The presentations of God's commands are continued in the narrative of events of Israel's history and the prophetic utterances which Israel experienced. The Old Testament was Israel's identity story.

God's commandments are always set within the narrative setting that traced Israel's existence. They are always addressed to concrete circumstances involving Israel. Divine commands are always addressed to actual situations; they are always *addressed* to living situations. They are given personally, as if God were one person and Israel were the other in dialogue with one another during an event in Israel's history. Even when they are mediated through a prophet, priest, judge, or king they appear addressed to all of Israel.

The prophetic books of the Old Testament all have their location in Israel's history, and what is prescribed by God through the prophets has both an immediate audience and a continuous application. Prophetic literature, such as Isaiah, incorporated not only the prophet's words that are a condemnation of the negative behavior of God's people, but also are a divine call to those people to be reconciled, to return to the relationships Israel has with God in the definitive narratives (Is. 1:18-19); and therefore His words are prescriptive messages.

In the prophetic books not only is God's righteousness expressed concretely, but also his promises. Often the prophetic books point out how Israel has sinned and what God would have the Israelites do. Both the commandments and the prophetic messages foretelling the future and what God is going to do with Israel are made public, for example (Is. 2:1-4; 8:1-15; 11: 1-9). The "good news" of the prophet is often celebrated by the writer in a hymn of praise (Is. 25:1-5) as Israel's relationship with God is reconciled. The entire narrative of the prophets is part of Israel's established identity in the past and future.

To understand the divine commands a reader must look at the context provided by the narrator of the circumstance for the giving of the commands. If God's commands are given in the narrative, it is because they are to be considered as an ongoing element of the narrative and essential to it. This is very clear in the New Testament Gospels. Divine directives are woven into the narrative about Jesus and his followers. When the divine instructions are given in the letters to the churches, they are addressed either to a church as whole or to individuals in a given congregation. The giving of God's prescriptive rules is either a part of the reader's given story or addressed to particular individuals who are to share them with other members of the churches in the prolonged constitutive narrative. In the Old Testament, although the recipient of God's instructions may not be clearly stated, the texts read as though they were addressed to God's prophet, to the people as a whole, or to some figure in the defining narrative.

The Bible statements of God's imperatives include more than criminal statues; they included instructions regarding cultic practices, the formation of personal identity, the nature of God's chosen community, ethical injunctions, and the treatment of strangers or persons who were not part of the covenant community. Again God's imperatives are usually given within the definitive historical narrative, or are themselves historical examples that help to make them clearly more definitive as prescriptions.

Although they are grounded within a historical setting, they are not limited to that particular situation. As God given directives, they apply to other times and places analogously. In chapter two we saw that a decision handed down from God to a prophet or priest was recorded in a book to be handed down to other generations to be continuously within the community of God's chosen people. The pronouncements of the kings were also written down since they were considered to be given to the king by God. They became a permanent feature of Israel's established narrative and law. The written form of these decisions given to the prophets, kings and priests were kept as God's Word, written into the record.

The process of handing down the divine imperatives of the Gospels in the New Testament is the same process. Eyewitnesses repeated what, where, and when they had seen and heard Jesus teach, and the Church wrote down the record and kept it as the definitive story of God's interaction with His community.

When God has spoken, those who heard what He said either repeated what they heard or wrote it down for posterity. Not the most common, but certainly one of the least questionable, are the direct commandments given by God through one of His representatives, a prophet. The

Decalogue, or Ten Commandments, is probably the best known. In the case of the Decalogue, God dictates the terms of righteous behavior to Moses who transcribes them and delivers them to God's people. The Decalogue, as written in Exodus 20, is followed by a series of ordinances and divine instructions. In the Bible's narrative they are statutes given historically within three months of the Exodus from Egypt (Exodus 19:1). These ordinances cover Israel's identity and its consecration to God, included the Ten Commandments. They are followed by injunctions concerning the treatment of slaves, the treatment of daughters, the punishments for various forms of murder, the abuse of one's parents, indemnity for personal injury and the injury of another person's property, and the penalty for the seduction of a virgin. They are established. There are also statutes commanding that sorceresses be killed, statues that require the death penalty for bestiality, and the destruction of a person who sacrifices to other Gods.

Divine ordinances and instruction in the Bible function very much like common law practices. They do not rest on a universal metaphysical truth, abstract principles, reason, or standard legal procedures. They are God's injunction generated out of living situations and serve as examples for similar or analogous events that follow. They form concrete prescriptions rather than abstract principles, laws of nature, or abstract mandates. They are not generalizations of reason from which particular cases may be determined. They are not the product of a group process, although they are underwritten by Israel's acceptance of them as God's guidance. Similar instruction may appear in a different form elsewhere, and be applied equally as well as in an analogous situation. A comparison of the Ten Commandments in Exodus 20 with similar commandments in Deuteronomy 5 that are given later in the desert sojourn shows both the similarity and difference of basically the same commandments. The Ten Commandments as they are recorded in Deuteronomy five (Deut. 5:6-22) are God's command, but they do not read the same as in Exodus twenty (Ex. 20:1-17). The Sabbath, for example, in Exodus twenty gives the reason for resting on the Sabbath as God rested from His work of creation on the seventh day. Deuteronomy five makes God's deliverance of Israel from Egypt the reason for keeping the Sabbath. The difference in the reading of the statues indicates that they were tied to specific events rather than universal imperatives and could be restated for other occasions and even superseded. Both the statutes and the narratives indicate what is pleasing and not pleasing to God.

In Genesis 23:20 God promises to send an angel (a messenger) before His people to guard them on the way and bring them to the place which He has prepared for them. The angel acts on God's behalf. While Israel is claiming the land, the ordinances of the Lord are highly personalized. Israel promises to obey all the laws that were given them by Moses and the angel; and the laws are sealed through the process of enacting a blood covenant, a bonding act (Ex. 24:4-8). The sealing of the laws was the process whereby they not only became established as binding statutes for the parties of the covenant, but they became established through a blood pledge. The blood covenant was Israel's ratification of their acceptance of God's commands unto death itself.

In Exodus what follows the blood covenant are the instructions for the formation of Yahweh's worship practices. Again the point which is being made here is that God's instructions were given in concrete and often less than ideal situations. Israel was to obey God's instructions because Israel knew their origin and the circumstance of their being given. Those sets of circumstances would make concrete God's instructions and would serve as a guide for all later generations of Israelites. The incorporation of the instructions within a definitive narrative established them both as authoritative and provided a concrete setting to contextualize them as pledged by Israel's life blood.

Statues, laws, and commandments are the recorded Word of God as it came to prophets, kings, and priestly courts, and are *established* by the fact that a prophet's words happen, a king records his rulings which come from God, and a judgment is established in the mouth of two witnesses who have been examined by the priests who wrote the decision down for future generations as prescriptive instructions.

The third form of God's prescriptive instructions is made up of precedents. Precedents act as practices which we use to secure our identity and to remain consistent in our life styles as children of God and Christians. A precedent is an authoritative instance, action, case, or statement that may serve as an example or justification in subsequent events and cases. Precedents carry a different weight than laws or commandments carry, and do not all carry the same quality of imperative. They are some times part of a religious code and are maintained to affirm or reaffirm one's relationship with God. Precedents are exemplary stories, parables, or events which are told within the established narrative and carry their weight from the narrative of which they are a part whether it is an exemplary act of a righteous person, an Old Testament prophet, Jesus, or a member of the Early Church. Precedents can be expressed, as instructions, exemplary stories, parables, or in citations from Israel's and the Church's definitive and constitutive narratives.

Precedents range in importance. Those that are part of establishing identity are basic, even sacramental. Precedents which reinforce one's general life style are important, but do not initiate a person's identity. Other precedents shape one's moral and ethical decisions and are addressed to particular actions and their place in one's religious life style.

The three most important precedents an Israelite undertakes to constitute his identity are circumcision, when he is recognized as a child of Abraham and thereby covenanted with God. The second precedent which defines him is his Bar Mitzvah, which usually takes place around puberty and through which he consciously and willfully accepts God's commandments. The third occurs at death when he repeats the prayer:

> My God and God of my fathers, accept my prayer...
> Forgive me for all the sins which I have committed in my life time...
> Accept my pain and suffering as atonement and forgive my wrongdoing for against You alone have I sinned....
> I acknowledge that my life and recovery depend on You.
> May it be Your will to heal me.
> Yet if You Have decreed that I should die of this affliction,
> May my death atone for all sins and transgressions which I have committed before You.
> Shelter me in the shadow, of Your wings.
> Grant me a share in the world to come.
> Father of orphans and Guardian of widows, protect my beloved family....
> Into your hand I commit my soul. You redeem me,
> O Lord God of Truth.
> Hear O Israel, the Lord is our God, The Lord alone.
> The Lord He is God.
> The Lord He is God.

The precedent is set for the individual because it is established in the community which also has its precedents which gives identity to all of the community's members. Among Jews these are the keeping of the Sabbath, the Passover seder, Shavuot or Pentecost, Sukkot or the Feast of Tabernacles, New Year (Rosh Hashanah), and Yom Kipper (The Day of Atonement). All of these precedents are derived from Israel's narrative as a people and serve to reinforce both the individual and the community in their identity. Two other festivals mark definitive aspects of Jewish life but they are derived from a later time in Jewish history; these are Hanukkah to commemorate the rededication of the temple by Judas Maccabee in 165 B.C. and the festival Purim that commemorates Esther's acts as they recorded in the Old Testament book that bears her name. These precedents are regulated to reaffirm one's life style each and every year.

In the Christian community these precedents are superseded in the work of Jesus Christ and the Church. For the Christian community there are two sets of precedents which serve to give identity to a Christian. In the Roman Catholic community there are seven such precedents known as the sacraments: Baptism, Communion, Confirmation, Penance, becoming a member of a Holy Order, Matrimony, and Extreme Unction (usually referred to in the present as Anointing of the Sick). In the New Testament only Baptism and Communion are mentioned in the constitutive narratives; consequently the Protestant Reformers reduced the number of Sacraments to those two. However, many of the Churches which practice infant Baptism strongly encourage those baptized in early childhood to confirm their Baptism as they become of age. However, they do not consider Confirmation a necessary sacrament. Only Circumcision in Judaism and Baptism in Christianity have the special status of establishing identity in their communities of practice, of being necessary to constituting an individuals identity. It is not often said, but to engage in these precedents as defining one's selfhood indirectly means the acceptance of the narratives from which they come and therefore tacitly accepting the Scriptures as a integral part of one's own story.

Apart from these major precedents the Scriptures hold many precedents that more or less shape the individual's life as a child of God and the sense of what is right and wrong and consistent with God's will. These precedents are usually expressed as parables, exemplary events, or moral stories. In the Old Testament the prophet Nathan tells David a story, a parable, about a poor man who had only a single lamb and loved it like his own child. But a rich man, who had many sheep, took the lamb from him and served it to a wayfarer. David was incensed at the rich man's behavior and was about to search him out and have him killed because he had no pity. Nathan tells David he is the man; for in spite of what God had done for David, David had manipulated the death of Uriah the Hittite in order to have Uriah's wife for himself (II Samuel 12:1-15). Parables of this sort appear throughout the Old Testament, but it is Jesus who uses them most effectively in the New Testament Gospels to proclaim precedents of righteousness.

The teachings in parables, especially in the Gospels, are clearly prescriptive statements. Although they are not stated as laws or statutes, when they are understood they call for righteous actions and consistency with in one's character. Jesus' parables related to the Kingdom of God in Matthew 13-51 are paralleled or further developed in Mk. 4:1-33, Lk. 8:4-16, 10:25-37, 13:6-9,18-20, 14:15-33, 15:3-17, 18:9-27, 20:9-18, 21:29-32, are not just information but have a prescriptive function. Take for example, the parable of the sower indicates that not every seed which the sower sows will bring forth fruit. Jesus explains it to the disciples:

> Now the parable is this: The seed is the word of God. The ones along the path are those who have heard; then the devil comes and takes away the word from their hearts, that they may not believe and be saved. And the ones on the rock are those who, when they heard the word, received it with joy; but these have no root, they believe for a while and in time of temptation fall away. And as for what fell among the thorns, they are those who hear, but as they go on their way they are choked by the cares and riches and pleasures of life, and their fruit does not mature. And as for that in the good soil, they are those who, hearing the word, hold fast in an honest and good heart, and bring forth fruit with patience (Lk. 8:11-15).

The prescriptive message of this parable is not in the form of a statute or command. It is implicit in the parable itself. It forms a precedent for understanding the reception of the Word of God.

In Matthew 25:1-14 Jesus told a parable about ten young women who went to meet the bridegroom. Five of them were foolish, and five of them wise. The five who were wise took flasks of oil for their lamps with them. When the bridegroom was delayed, they all slept. Around midnight the cry went out that the bridegroom was coming, and they all trimmed their lamps. But the lamps of those five who had not taken extra oil did not have enough oil to keep their lamps lit, nor did they have time to go get more. When they finally returned from getting oil and asked to enter the wedding feast the master said to them that he did not know them. The imperative in this parable is clear; it was the precedent to be prepared for the coming of the Kingdom. All of the parables recorded in Matthew twenty-five about the coming of the kingdom set the precedent of preparedness.

Some precedents are not parables but are events pointed out from everyday life that carry an imperative and are recorded in the Scriptures. Their authority rests on the communities' understanding of the source of their directive force. Mark's Gospel recalls an event that took place opposite the treasury in Jerusalem:

> And he (Jesus) sat down opposite the treasury, and watched the multitude putting money in the treasury. Many rich people put in large sums. And a poor widow came, and put in two copper coins, which make a penny. And he called his disciples to him, and said to them, "Truly, I say to you this poor widow has put in more than all those who are contributing to the treasury. For they all contributed out of their abundance; but she out of her poverty has put in everything she had, her whole living."(Mk. 2:41-44)

This narrative became a precedent when it was *established* in the Church as part of what Jesus said and did. Notice how difficult it would have been to make this a commandment, or a principal based on reason or some metaphysical reality. It carries with it all the authority of a law, but it is not expressed like a law.

When we move to the Old Testament and look at the story of Abraham and Isaac, we get another event as a precedent; one that has to do with Abraham's faith in God. In the precedent God tells Abraham to take his only son Isaac whom he loves to Mount Moriah and God will show him a mountain where he is to offer Isaac as a burnt offering. According to the precedent, Abraham followed God's instructions; and on the third day out from their home Abraham saw the place that he was to sacrifice Isaac, and dismissed the two servants who were with them. Then Abraham proceeded to the place, took the wood that he had cut and laid it on Isaac's back. Abraham took in his own hand the fire and the knife to sacrifice Isaac. As the two proceed, Isaac asks his father where is the lamb that is to be sacrificed. Abraham answers him, "God will provide the lamb for a burnt offering, my son." When they arrived at the place that God showed Abraham, he builds an altar. places the wood on the altar, and ties Isaac to the alter. When Abraham took the knife to kill his son, an angel of the Lord calls to him, "Do not lay your hand on the lad or do anything to him; for now I know that you fear God...." Abraham saw a ram caught in the thicket by its horns and offered it up to God instead of Isaac. Abraham called the place, "The Lord will provide." The text states that the place was from then on called, "On the mount of the Lord it shall be provided" (Gen. 22:1-14). And again God blesses Abraham and says: "... and by your descendants shall all the nations of the earth bless themselves, because you have obeyed my voice" (Gen 22:18). The precedent calls the reader to faithfulness, because God will provide, and to hope, because God has promised. The Abraham narrative is not an imperative for everyone wishing to serve God, but it becomes an example of trust in God and God's response.

Precedents deal with how some biblical *events* themselves have been used normatively to prescribe, to justify, or condemn behavior which is analogous with other events. These *events* are not statutes or laws, but precedents which can be used at any analogous time to determine or enact God's will. For example, what David does with the bread of the Presence in the tabernacle when he is hungry becomes an example of a contingency which allows someone to break the Sabbath laws (I Sam. 21:1-6; Mk. 2:23-28).

Prescriptive narratives, precedence, often shape our understanding of our obligation to fulfill righteousness. The story of Ananias and Sapphira, who lied about their gifts to God (Acts 5:1-11), is a precedent event concerning the proper way to make one's offering. Other such narratives are the account that Abraham after the defeat of Chedorlaomer gives to

Melchizadek, king of Salem, a tithe (Gen. 14:14-18). It sets the paradigm for the tithe. Joseph's forgiving his brothers in Egypt (Gen. 45:1-15) is a normative precedents but in a different way than a statute. These examples are not different in the normative quality which they express. They are not universal laws, but precedents set for the life of the individuals and the people of God. They are not universal laws but they are prescriptive by analogy; they are paradigms of righteousness and unrighteousness.

One of the central themes of the Scriptures is the bonding of God's people with one another. Circumcision was not simply an act to establish one's identity as a child of Abraham; it was a covenantal bonding act with God (Gen. 17:9-10). Throughout the Old Testament bonding acts are used to establish bonds between people committed to one another. One such precedent is the relationship between Ruth and Naomi which was strengthened by Ruth's words to her mother-in-law. "Entreat me not to leave you or return from following after you; for where you go I will go, and where you lodge I will lodge; your people shall be my people, and your God my God; where you die I will die, and there will I be buried" (Ruth 1:16-17a).

The precedent of Jonathan's covenant making with David is similar (I Sam.18:1-5). In the New Testament the participation in the Lord's Supper in which the flesh and blood of the Messiah are remembered till his coming, is both a bonding act and an act that establishes one's covenant identity (I Cor.1:23-33). Reading Scripture as one's own story is itself an act of bonding with others who read in the same manner,

Another form of precedent is a *narrative* or *story* in the Scriptures that is used as a directive. Each pericope that can be used as an example of what one should do or not do, say or not say, in situations that are analogous to the text is a precedent. The narratives which are used as a precedent are prescriptive because they have divine authority. Like the commandments and statues they are not based on a political or philosophical theory but on God's action or God's initiative. Precedents are very concrete, very existential. Precedents are prescriptive as *part of the narrative of God's acts among His people* and their responses to Him and to one another. They are part of the *established* Word of God.

The narratives are normative because they are the established recorded Word of God. The narratives are first of all purported to be the record of events which they describe, i.e., history. But they serve as more than history, they are *normative examples* as well. It is not enough to establish their historical accuracy; they are normative when they are read or addressed as prescriptive accounts to guide the reader or hearer in what they should do in analogous situations. They are not in the form of a statute. When they are used as precedents, they are prescriptive accounts taken from parts of the story of God's activity and the actions (or lack of action) that people demonstrated in their responses to God's activity; they become *paradigms* for righteousness or unrighteousness.

The Garden of Eden narrative begins by describing God as the creator of the world. The purpose of the narratives is to show the greatness of Israel's God as the creator. These narratives are not science; they are descriptions of the power and nature of Israel's God. The lessons of the narratives are not about ontology or cosmology, but about the greatness of Israel's God to create out of nothing. The fact that there are two different narratives about how God creates in Genesis one and two does not diminish the greatness of God. Once the greatness of God is laid out, the narrative tells of God's relationship with Adam and Eve. Humankind has a chosen idyllic relationship with God. Evil is introduced to the story and leads to Adam's and Eve's disobedience to God and the consequences. It serves as a prescriptive archetype or precedent that warns readers of the consequence of disobeying the Creator God and breaking one's relationship with God through disobedience. It personifies with Satan the temptation to disbelieve God and enhance one's own status. In the New Testament Paul uses the first chapters of Genesis to characterize the first Adam and the second Adam. He draws on the power of the Genesis story to indicate God's new defining work in the second Adam. What he says about the New Adam would make no sense at all if it were not for the precedent of the first Adam (Romans 5:12-14). The second Adam is drawn into the identity defining story of God's people by treating Him as the necessary sequel to the initial narrative.

To get bogged down in determining the historic accuracy of the creation narratives is to overlook their primary purpose as normative discourse. The accounts are normative because they tell of God's greatness, and His relation to Adam and Eve, and the break down of the relationship of God with His people. The narrative precedents are normative because they were perceived as archetypes of God's activity and human behavior which was displeasing to God. The great and powerful God seeks a relationship with His creation and human kind immediately spoils that relationship. The paradigm can be applied to every human's behavior when a question arises about the merits of what one chose to do.

When the entire historical episode forms the imperative, it is not limited to its immediate narrative context. It is especially true with events which are examples of righteousness. Those events are not limited to their initial enactment, but like common law practices they are applicable by analogy to other events.

In the second chapter we saw that the statutes were given by the prophets to address particular issues and that the judgments of the kings were not generalizations but decisions about particular issues written down to be used for cases that were analogous to them. Both the statues and the narratives were drawn up to deal with specific issues. The statutes were specific with regard to their content. The narratives were also descriptive of particular events. The applications for both were by analogy rather than the application of some sort of categorical imperative, or a universal law of either nature or reason. Unlike modern ethical statements, they address particular events and are applied by analogy. None of them is derived from reasoning or from natural law.

As persons identify with the statutes and the narratives, they learned a common righteousness. To live as though the statutes and narratives determined one's life was to discover one's meaning in life and one's self-understanding. Someone who visualized himself as standing in the same line of history as the Fathers, saw himself as both a child of Adam and Eve and also Abraham, and consequently obliged to be obedient to the laws given to Moses. To read the New Testament as one's own book is to bond with other persons who do the same. To live by the statutes and the precedents is to live by righteousness. To claim the narratives as one's own story and to live by the statutes was to truly live a life pleasing to God.

If a reader of the Scriptures wants to get the most from the narratives of the Bible he needs to claim the Bible narratives as the story of his ancestors, his own roots. Just as a person recounts the stories of his family ancestors, their origin and the events that make them distinctively who they are, Scripture when it is adopted as the story of one's ancestors provides a genuine framework for a person to shape his own character in the ways of his people. In the case of choosing the Bible as one accessorial story one chooses righteousness and a walk with God. Psalms 119 is a song about keeping God's ordinances in one's heart that one might not sin against God (Ps. 119:11).

Reading Christian Scripture is more than simply reading another story book or history book; one reads in order that the story becomes part of one's consciousness. To read the Scriptures in this manner is to submerge oneself in the narrative and consciously or unconsciously claim it for one's self. The reading of the Bible as one's own story and the story of one's true ancestors makes the way of life concrete. The creedal repetition of a Biblical story tends to make it abstract. Narratives shared as common stories keep their subliminal and personal appeal. When we objectify these narratives and distance them as an object to study and verify, we often kill their appeal to our self identity. They often lose their simple directness that leads us to righteousness.

Reading the Scriptures as precedents not only shapes one's own identity, but it bonds us with others who share the same identity. When the precedents of the Scriptures are held in common in a community they serve as a bond between the members of the community. They shape the community's identity and sense of solidarity. We do not normally see that reading the Scriptures with other persons as a bonding process, but in fact it gives to the community a common source for its sense of righteousness.

Precedents which make up our identity are usually put into actions or words which not only express our own self-understanding, but also set forth the self- understanding of other members of the Church; and we pick them up by conviction or because we experience other people doing similar things. We carry them around in our memory. We are not particularly aware of them until some one points them out. Their statute becomes obvious when our attention is turned toward them. They are meaningful to us because we are heirs of biblical culture, and the life of the Church. They are not particularly spiritually meaningful to those who stand outside the biblical narrative examining them without having claimed them as one's own story.

Some precedents are part of our community's calendar or part of the social expectations which are reinforced by reenacting them. Israel's ritual calendar was based on the covenantal narrative precedents. The practice of celebrating Christmas and Easter served the same purpose in the Church. Participating in Communion on a regular basis reinforces the place that Christ's death, burial, and covenant play in the lives of Christians.

Notice that the previously mentioned prescriptions are not in the form of legal statues. In the Scriptures self-understanding, bonding, and moral precedents are usually set out in a narratives. Some are addressed to us as sermons or teaching, or sent to us as admonitions in a letter. They are also set out in declarations and moral instructions. The narratives and the declarations are set out for the reader as normative precedents are analogous to our daily life. Interpreting precedence for the life of the Church requires that there be an understanding of them as a type of imperative claim. There are customs within institutions and communities that determine the use of precedence which need to be recognized when we apply them to our self-understanding and use them within the contemporary Church. When the historical episode forms the imperative, it is not limited to its immediate narrative context. It is especially true with events which are examples of righteousness. Those events are not limited to their initial enactment, but like common law practices they are applicable by analogy to other events.

Again what are precedents? By definition a precedent is an established account of a prescriptive narrative, action, or statement concerning the correctness of specific behavior used as a normative guide for belief or action in subsequent circumstances that are analogous.

Precedent actions are often reinforced by stories or contained in our communal narratives because they have been given to us in order to lead us to enact given practices. Many of the narratives of the Scriptures carry the weight of defining who we are, to whom we belong, and what we should do. Precedent actions, sacraments, and other forms of prescribed righteousness take on their meaning in the recitation of the story of which they are a part.

A precedent is only a precedent if it is *established* in the use of a community, or is an *established* record of a definitive event for a given community. It must be accepted as a given among its users. When a precedent is established in a moral, religious, or legal setting, it functions as a normative phenomenon. A precedent is not a mere telling of a story, but the *use* of the narrative or event (or a statement about it) as a normative guide to action.

Precedents never exhaust all of the existential dimensions of the event or saying they represent. As narratives, they are second-order prescriptive phenomena which take on a life of their own when they are adopted, either formally or informally, into the customs and traditions of a community. When a precedent is established or set, it operates within the moral or legal system which functions beyond the particular events or statements that are narrated in the precedents.

A precedent serves as an irreducible given in the community which uses it. It may be accompanied by an explanation, but it cannot be explained away or rendered meaningless through some form of reductionism or abstract commentary. A precedent statement is generated within an existential setting and reflects the decisive nature of that situation for the future of those who use the preserved precedent normatively. For example, common law marriage is a precedent in American Common Law. Common law practices are usually based on a well *established common practice* within a community. It may be based on earlier court decisions that were recorded, but not codified as law.

A precedent is first established by common usage within the community. When it is recorded into a legal system, it is re-established or placed there by actions taken by a governing body under fairly restrictive rules. Once established either as common practice or as part of the legal code of a governing body, it is decisive for future adjudication of the law in relevant matters.

Precedents are statements which originate out of a given setting. In most cases precedents which are set during an event do not describe the event in detail because the more detailed the circumstances stated in the precedent, the less its applicability by analogy to subsequent situations. Once a precedent is accepted, it is applied by analogy to other situations. The analogical nature of the precedent is limited if it can be understood only in circumstances that are identical to the original context in which it was formed. Few, if any, subsequent contexts are going to replicate in detail the context in which a precedent is found in the Scriptures or elsewhere. Times change, and precedents apply by analogy to new events. In this sense the precedent is freed from its original historical and sociological setting. This is one reason that super-session is possible in the Bible. Attempting to adjudicate a judgment from the setting of a precedent by explaining it in terms of its historical or social origins makes the precedent difficult or impossible to use because its analogical function is limited to the narrow context of the initial circumstance. Biblical precedents rested on the fact that they are established, community's precedents authorized by God, to be applied in any analogous event, and neither the time of their occurrence nor the immediate social understanding limits their prescriptive nature.

Precedents which are incorporated into the traditions of the society take on a reality of their own; they become cultural artifacts which are in force as long as they are considered established in their communities or are superseded by a higher righteousness. It is precisely the ability of the wording of the precedent to be applied to new and different circumstances that makes them a powerful prescriptive tool. They have a meaning which is not reducible to any given context in which they have been previously applied. Because precedents are applied to situation analogous to the one in which they are generated, they are not like statements of unchanging, universal truths, or principles and laws which govern all situations regardless of the place or time. Again, precedents are not based on the laws of nature or on a universal metaphysical reality derived by reason. A precedent may be part of a collection of precedents or be part of a sequence of precedents dealing with a common topic, but they are not grounded in either nature or reason. They are grounded in memory and texts of the community which holds them to be normative.

The community that recorded the life and teachings of Jesus incorporated a series of both sayings and narratives which had not been given before. Jesus' use of parables epitomizes the formation of precedents. The historical material which makes up the gospels does not exhaust the meaning of the narratives. What is said and done by Jesus becomes the common basis of the Church and prescribes what the life of a follower of Jesus should be like. Jesus gave few statues, but he gave numerous precedents in both what he said and what he did. From the narratives of Jesus' birth to the reports of the resurrection the Gospels are full of precedent behavior and sayings.

Steven's sermon in Acts 7:1-59 is an identity precedent, which the

Church knew to be its own. Insofar as the Church preached the life, death, and resurrection of Jesus they were setting out the basic identity precedent for the Church. Whatever statues may have been laid down, none of them carried the weight of the narrative of Jesus life, death, and resurrection. The inclusion of Gentiles into the community of the called is prescribed to the Early Church through the narratives of Peter's vision and his subsequent actions. (Acts 10:1-48).The precedent rest solely on God's initiative.

It really is no wonder that the Book of Revelation is also a vision composed of narratives that set the precedents for the end times. Looking at the narratives of the New Testament for their historical value alone often misses their normative, performative function.

---

[1] J.L. Austin, <u>How To Do Things With Words</u>, ed. J.O. Urmson, Oxford University Press, New York, 1970.

CHAPTER V

Consequential Meaning and Performative Language

1. CONSEQUENTIAL MEANING IN THE SCRIPTURES

Although there is not a formal language theory expressed in the Bible, there is an implicit understanding of the use of some forms of language to achieve given consequences. The writers of both the Old and New Testament accepted the fact that some language had performative consequence; that is, the use of language caused things to happen. Whether we deem their understanding of what they were doing as accurate or faulty, nevertheless it determined the way that language was used to communicate in that linguistic community.

Whether one is reading the creation narratives in Genesis or the Logos narrative in the Fourth Gospel, God speaks and His Word creates the physical universe. The creative and sustaining power of language often takes on a life of its own. When a statement is uttered or written, for example, a blessing or a curse, the force of the language remains in effect, and it may or may not be revoked depending on the circumstances. When Isaac is deceived by Jacob and gives Jacob the blessing which was intended for Esau, Isaac cannot revoke the blessing, and has to bless Esau with another lesser blessing (Gen. 27:1-40).

We have already seen how the words of a prophet are authenticated as the Word of God by the coming to pass of that which is spoken by the prophet. The prophet's words do more than predict the future; as the Word of God they create the future. The biblical writers did not think that all language carried consequential force; they set out very few explicit rules as to what language had consequential force. What is available to us are examples of usage and narratives about language usage that give us clues to their linguistic understanding and practices.

In the second chapter of I Corinthians Paul makes a very clear distinction between language which is the product of human wisdom and the message which he preached through the power of the Spirit. Paul claims that only the Spirit knows the mind of God and is capable of revealing the secret wisdom of God to those who have ears to hear. The transforming power of Paul's preaching has the language of the Spirit as it source.

The understanding of performative language or consequential use of language is not limited to language's ability to create and transform, but also involves the role a person plays in the naming process and the functions which names themselves play. To know the name of something, or to give something a name, was to exercise power over it. Names incorporate that identity of the object or person named. Often in the Bible if a person's basic identity changes so does his name. Abram's name is changed to Abraham; Jacob's to Israel; Saul's to Paul. A new name is indicative of a new role in life or a new character.

When we go through the Scriptures we can find examples of the writer's understanding of the consequential effects of language usage. Adam exercises his dominion over the world by naming the other creatures. By naming the other creatures Adam relates himself to them. That which is taken out of his own being he names "woman," indicating that the union between a man and his wife involves a shared dominion of the earth and takes precedence over parental relationships.

In some cases the presence of a name had ontological implications; the object named was considered to have a real presence where the name was uttered or written. The name of a person and his being are inseparably bound together. The place where God puts His name or causes His name to dwell is the place where God Himself is present (Deut. 12:5, 11, 21; I Kg. 8:48; II Chron. 6:1-11). In the ancient world people often inscribed their names on rocks so that their names "Would not be blotted from the face of the earth." To have one's name blotted out was to cease to exist (Deut. 29:20). Immortality was to have one's name remembered or continued. It was so important in Israel that one's name not be blotted out from the face of the earth that when a man died without children to carry on his name, then his next oldest brother was to marry the man's widow and name the first child after the deceased. Levirate marriage was a way to guarantee that a person's name not disappear from Israel (Deut. 25:5-10). In the book of Ruth, when Elimelech dies, he leaves his wife Naomi and two sons, Mahon and Chilion. The two sons marry, but they die before they have offspring. Naomi decides to return from the land of Moab to her home in Israel. She is too old to have children, but she encourages her two daughters-in-law to stay in Moab and raise families. One daughter-in-law does this, but Ruth returns to Israel with her mother-in-law. She gleans in the fields of Elimelect's kinsman Boaz; and eventually, after some intrigue, he wants her as his wife. However, the nearest kinsman has a right to Ruth before Boaz. Boaz approaches the nearest kinsman and asks him if he will redeem Elimelech's land and with it Ruth. The nearest kinsman declines to be the redeemer, and Boaz redeems Elimelect's property and takes Ruth to be his wife. Boaz says to the elders and the people.

> You are witnesses this day that I have bought from the hand of Naomi all that belonged to Elimilech and all that belonged to Chilion and Mahlon. Also Ruth the Moabitess, the widow of Mahlon, I have bought to be my wife, to perpetuate the name of the dead in his inheritance, that the name of the dead may not be cut off from among his brethren and from the gate of his native place: you are witnesses this day (Ruth 4:9-10).

Ruth, a non-Israelite, becomes a heroine because she is the instrument through whom Elimelech's name is perpetuated. The mother of Obed, the father of David, saved the family name from being cut off from Israel.

To share or take on another's name was to be united with the other parties who bear the shared name. This was very much like the later western practice when a son was adopted he took his adopted father's name; and in marriage a women took her husband's name. To take someone's name was no trifling matter. When Israel enters into covenant with Yahweh, Yahweh causes His name to dwell among them (Deut. 26:2). They took Yahweh's name that was given to them. The commandment, "You shall not take the name of the Lord your God in vain; for the Lord will not hold him guiltless who takes His name in vain," is a commandment against taking on God's name through covenanting and then becoming an apostate or acting hypocritically (Ex. 20:7). The command is not a commandment against cursing; responsible cursing is widely used in Scripture. The command is an injunction against unfaithfulness.

To take on a person's name was to share in his or her identity. Consequently when the Early Church baptized into the name of the Father, Son, and Holy Spirit, they were baptizing persons into union with the Godhead (Matt. 28:19). To call on the name of the Lord was to engage God in the task at hand. It was a process of invoking God's intervention and action to address an immediate set of circumstances. It was very much like our current attachment of the words, "So help me God," to an oath. It engaged God in what was being said and done.

The statement, "There is no other name under heaven given among men whereby you must be saved," is both a claim for the name Jesus Messiah, but more significantly for the uniqueness of Jesus Messiah (Acts 4:12). It is also true that when prayers are uttered in Jesus' name, his presence and power are invoked (John 14:13). It is not a simple matter of calling on God's name with Jesus' name as an endorsement. It was praying as participating in Jesus Christ through his name.

The use of the power of a name is illustrated in Mk. 9:38 when a nonfollower of Jesus was casting out demons in Jesus' name. When the disciples objected, Jesus declared that kindness shown to those who bear his name will not go un-rewarded. To be called a Christian was to take on the identity of the Christ as one's own identity.

In both Testaments names are inseparable from the being of that which is named. The name was the very identity of that which was named. In Philippians Jesus is given a name above every name, "that at His name every knee should bow in heaven and on earth and under the earth, and every tongue confess that Jesus Christ is Lord, to the glory of God, the Father" (Phil. 2:9-11). Not only does this passage indicate Jesus' elevation, but it also calls for a confession by all persons of Jesus status. To make that confession was not only an acknowledgement and affirmation of Christ's personal Lordship over the speaker, but it was to be the culminating event in the realization of that Lordship in the cosmic order.

To control a name is in fact to control that which is named. Consequently Israel never used Yahweh's name, because it was blasphemous to do so. According to the Noah accounts, human beings lose part if their power when they lose control over language. In their desire not to be scattered over the face of the earth, they wished "to make a name for themselves" by building a city and a tower which reached to heaven (Gen. 11:4). To make a name for one's self was to exalt one's self. The Genesis narrative states:

> And the Lord came down to see the city and the tower, which
> the sons of men had built. And the Lord said, "Behold, they are
> one people, and they have all one language; and this is only the
> beginning of what they will do; and nothing that they propose to do
> will now become impossible for them. Come, let us go down, and
> confuse their language, that they may not understand one another's
> speech" (Gen. 11:5-7).

The New Testament sequel to this event occurs at Pentecost. The people are gathered from all over the face of the earth and they hear, each in his own tongue. A name has been given to them that will empower them. In explaining the phenomenon to the crowds Peter says that not only are the words of the prophets fulfilled in the pouring out of God's Spirit upon His people, but "... it shall be that whoever calls on the name of the Lord shall be saved" (Acts 2:21). The people are not saving themselves though making a name for themselves, but a name is given to them whereby they will be saved.

It is clear that in the symbolic world of the Scriptures naming and the use of names was not a trivial matter. The use and misuse of language is a major factor in the very manner in which humans related to God, themselves, and the world.

The Scriptures use numerous linguistic genres which are associated with performative functions and therefore have consequential meaning. Vows, promises, covenants, testament (wills), commandments, songs, admonitions, laments, warnings, narratives, apocalyptic passages, etc., are all used to communicate an intended action or cause a given response in the hearer or reader. As interpreters of the Scriptures in the contemporary world, we are in a better position to explicate how these genres communicate and detail the rules and skills which make it possible to use them effectively.

In 1955 J. L. Austin delivered the William James Lectures at Harvard University; they were later published as <u>How</u> <u>to</u> <u>Do</u> <u>Things</u> <u>With</u> <u>Words</u>.[1] Taking his cue from Ludwig Wittgenstein, Austin began to examine the way we use language other than to describe objects of our experience. By saying something we often do more than merely describe events; we actually perform an action which has consequences in our world. There are consequences that occur from uttering statements, just as there are consequences of our other actions. For example, when we declare war against another country the status and condition of the two states is quite different. When we bequeath our property to someone through a will, we have caused an event to occur. When we enter contracts, those contracts are binding and determine our subsequent behavior. Austin called these types of utterances performative; that is they do not merely describe the action which they imply, they do it. In performative language content and significance are employed to provide results, consequences.

Biblical scholars have long recognized that the Bible contained performative language. H. Wheeler Robinson not only acknowledged the power of language in God's act of creation, he also recognized the power of God's word spoken by a prophet.[2] In the New Testament Paul claims in I Cor. 2:1-5 that he was not preaching with words of wisdom but with the power of the Holy Spirit. The power and force of language was not invented by Austin, but his works are helpful in understanding the use of language in the Scriptures.

Performative utterances and written statements have rules and procedures which a language community follows when it effectively uses them. As far as we know the Bible writers had no such formal rules which they taught one another. We can only draw from the uses they employed in the language of their writings. The rules are often unspoken by the users of a language. However, if these rules are followed, the consequences of their usage and function are understood and there are appropriate responses. For example, suppose two people were getting married. Although the same words may be used at the rehearsal that are used in the actual wedding itself, they are not effective apart from the proper setting, the proper licensing, the proper people, the proper attitude of the couple, and the proper context. However, when the words, "I do." are said under the proper conditions and proper authority, the wedding become legally, socially, and personally binding. They may be divorced or widowed, but their real status in society is changed by the ceremony and its language.

Performative statements, uttered or written under the respective rules which are determined by the language community which uses them, have consequences.[3] These consequences are more or less predictable because they follow rules which determine the manner in which they are articulated and their usage. They are also more or less predictable because they depend upon the skill of the speaker or writer to articulate them appropriately to a given audience. Sometimes the consequences fail because they are simply misspoken or miscommunicated by their author or misunderstood or misappropriated by those to whom the communication is addressed. Not everyone in a given language community communicates equally well.

Unexpected consequences may occur when authors do not anticipate the results of their statements. Either they are not fully aware of the context in which their statements are made, and do not follow the community rules for the use of the performative language which they are employing, or because they are misinterpreted by the hearer/reader.

Not only can statements be misspoken or misunderstood, they can be consciously declined or refused. What is written or declared can be obviated by those who refuse to respond, or respond poorly, to the use of the statements in their socially regulated way. The fact that commands can be disobeyed does not keep them from functioning as directives or imperatives. The fact that a contract can be broken does not keep it from being in effect. This recognition that language can accomplish something, that it has consequences, is closely akin to the way ancient Israel used language.

Sometimes a given performative genre can be used for more than one consequence. Generally speaking a given performative genre will be used in a manner that is commensurate with the grammatical and linguistic constructs of the statement. However, communities of users often use a given genre in more than one way. We shall see examples of this multi-dimensional use when we look at the use of law as prescriptive language. The specific consequence of the use of a genre depends upon the community's acceptance of that use and its determination of the proper performance of the language act.

Interpreting the Bible as Scripture for the life of the Church often has been limited to tell what the referential meaning of the text states or describes. Telling the referential meaning of a text has its appropriate place where information alone is being sought. However, when the text is being used to shape the life of the Church, a more complete communication of the text's meaning involves interpreting it in such a way that the performative or consequential function of the test is also communicated as an imperative, not simply as a description of what was an imperative in the past. If a covenant is being interpreted to a contemporary audience as a bonding statement addressed to the audience, it needs to be conveyed as a promise, not merely a record of past events and sayings. Covenants are the authoritative language of the Church which creates and continues the identity, hopes, life style, and moral actions of the community. Interpreting the full meaning of a biblical text includes restating the referential content of the passage, its significance, and the use of the language which produces consequences.

In order to identify the use of a given Biblical statement and its consequential meaning it is helpful to begin by setting out a tentative typology of performative usage.

The following list is tentative for two reasons: (1) the list does not exhaust the possible types of performative statements or consequences. Several other performative functions such as play, humor, and pornography are also possible, but they have limited or no application to biblical texts. (2) The different types which are listed are not mutually exclusive. There are times when the consequences of a statement can elicit more than one consequence.

In the Scriptures there are descriptive and informative statements, but all of them serve more than an objective presentation of their referents. Strictly speaking there are no purely scientific statements in the Bible which are communicated only for the sake of their referents. In the Scriptures when we find descriptive, analytical statements, clarification statements or explanations, they are always communications which are meant to illicit a response from the hearer/reader. To look at the Scriptures purely as objective information is to fail to understand the consequential nature of what is being communicated. This does not mean that the writers do not attempt to convey what they consider "facts" (that which is established) to be, but it means that the "facts" always are communicated in order to evoke a consequence.

The following categories are six general types of performative statements that can be broken down into more specific language events, but they broadly outline the primary types of performative language used in the Scriptures: (1) constituting, (2) bonding, (3) expressing, (4) exalting, (5) transforming, and (6) comforting and blessing.

A. CONSTITUTIVE LANGUAGE

Constitutive language may be expressed in a number of different ways. Constitutions, the rules of monastic orders, creeds, and confessions are clear forms of constitutive language, but the constitutive language of some communities is stated in narratives, legends, traditions, and myths. Constitutive language is always social in that it defines the horizons or parameters of a social unit and the individuals which make up that grouping. It is language which shapes identity and self-understanding. It provides an external, foundational linguistic guide that gives both a common denominator for the members of a community and a basis for individual and social stability and continuation. In the previous chapter we saw how precedents serve a constitutive role as well as a directive or prescriptive function.

Constitutive language may also be the source of the formation of social institutions within the community that uses it. Constitutive language is often the source of cultural artifacts such as ritual, literature, art, sculpture, architecture, governing institutions, and legal structures. The institutions and cultural artifacts become embodiments of the constitutive language, much like American democratic institutions become space-time embodiments of the American Constitution.

The claim that certain forms of religious language usage shape, create, and sustain a given social order and the people within them is not new. Berger, Luckman, and Geertz said this some time ago.[4] George Linbeck makes a good case for dogma serving as the constitutive basis for consensus in a given religious community.[5] There is no single way in which a given statement, set of statements, dialogues, or narratives become constitutive for a given group or individuals. A community or a person may deliberately choose a set of constitutive statements such as a constitution, but often constitutive statements, particularly constitutive narratives, hang together loosely and unsystematically as the background for our consciousness. It is not necessary that persons even be focally aware that a given set of statements are constitutive for them. Our tacit awareness and acceptance of the language shapes our choices and behavior. Open acceptance of constitutive statements gives them greater force and stability, but it also makes them more accessible to analysis and criticism.

Constitutive language becomes habituated for us; we incorporate its significance so that it gives us a place in the world. Narrative constitutive language functions to place us both diachronically and synchronically. Diachronically it gives us a sense of origin and connection with the past, a history, or a tradition, and it give us connections with other people and communities that share the same or similar constitutive language within the extended bound of our current understanding of the world. Synchronically it gives us a place in a given time.

Constitutive language is more immediate than our world-view in that it defines our place within the whole. A world-view is an inclusive understanding of the universe which is embedded in our culture and linguistic structures. Constitutive language shapes our unique identity and selfunderstanding within our world-view, and these processes are often acquired before we have any critical distance to what we hear, read, or see.

As constitutive language there are statements which provide us with stability through changing circumstances; they provide a durability to those situations in which one may be swept away or caught up in that which runs fundamentally against our "true" nature.

There are some people who consciously craft their constitutive claims and consciously adopt a set of constitutive statements to define their selfhood and place in the world. For most of us the process is a tacit process, i.e. we hear, read, or see something over a period of time and it becomes habituated as part of our make up. On a community level the process is the same. Some communities have a critical distance to the process of stating defining claims, and may withhold acceptance until they can deliberately adopt a constitutive statement or statements. They may write constitutions or develop a confession or set of creeds as definitive of themselves and their communities. Not uncommonly, however, in the process of self-definition and community identity formation, previously held tacit constitutive factors will filter into the new constructions

Constitutive language can lose its force and consequential meaning. It can be deconstructed, destroyed, forgotten, replaced, or become transparent. The objective analysis of their constitutive language can cause people to distance themselves from the force and acceptance of their own constitutive language. When this happens their constitutive language goes transparent and they tend to choose other statements as their basis of self-understanding. There is nothing to guarantee the perpetual force of constitutive meaning but its continued usage by the society, its institutions, and the individuals who embody it in their lifestyles.

The consequences of the use of constitutive language are that individuals and communities are differentiated by what they have adopted or absorbed. Regardless of how vague or well-defined, complex or simple the constitutive language is, it becomes the matrix from which people live out their identity and find their place. Within the Bible the narrative sections set out for the Jewish and Christian communities are the most fundamental constitutive materials. In the Old Testament the Pentateuch, or Torah, is the dominant constitutive material which is further elaborated through time by the historical books Joshua, Judges, I and II Kings, I and II Chronicles, Ezra, and Nehemiah. Books like Jonah, Ruth, and Esther further illustrate what is central to the defining features of the central narratives. In story form they further refine the constitutive message of the central narrative. The prophetic books of the Old Testament enrich episodes and episodic periods in the definitive narrative. The Psalms repeat the refrains in song, and the wisdom literature provides practical wisdom to those who are already defined by the narratives as God's people.

In the New Testament the Gospels and Acts serve much the same function, i.e., the narratives about Jesus and the Early Church are constitutive for the community and individual Christian. The narratives are full of precedents that reflect the character of the community which is rooted in the story. It is the Church's story, regardless of whoever else claims it or dismisses it. The Epistles derive their significance as follow up expressions of the life of Jesus Christ and the Early Church and serve as interpretation and expansion of the basic narrative.

The narratives provided both Jewish and Christian communities with an understanding of their origins and diachronic development. The narratives set out the history of God's activity in relationship to the community and the individuals who share in the tradition. These narratives not only encompass the past, but also spell out the community's ever reviving hope for the future and the ends of human life. They are a saga of human existence with its primary referent centered in God's action with His people. The defining portrait of a people, a community which arises out of the narrative is of people chosen by God for a unique life lived together with God. This image shapes both the individual's life and gives geographic extension to the community which takes the narrative as constitutive of their life and identity. It differentiates both the individual and the community from the rest of the world.

What is unique about the Biblical narrative is that it is composed of vignettes, pericopes, individual units, which are strung together on a timeline which is irregular in terms of real time. There are major focal events; there are sidebars; there are chronicles which appear to follow real time; and there are anomalies and duplications. Nevertheless the narratives have finality about them. As a whole they form a backdrop for the directing, bonding, expressing, exalting, transforming, and enabling language which is embedded in them and parallel to them.

One of the characteristics of Biblical constitutive narratives is that individual episodes can be used as definitive precedents for understanding a future event, or as a basis for adjudicating other forms of consequential statements. At the same time the narratives can be seen as a progression of understanding and can be modified to fit new circumstances. The significance of particular narratives can be used to interpret both past and new constitutive understanding. Because the past promises were made pointing to a new and different future, the meaning of some events takes on a different significance as their recall unfolds. New precedents follow old precedence, and often a recall unfolds. The precedent follows old precedents, and often there must be an adjudication of constitutive language to determine the significance of both the older and newer statements because the identity of the community and its behavior depend upon the outcome. In the Bible constitutive language is not ossified into an absolute timeless code, but a living and growing tradition associated with the acts of God with His chosen people in which new narratives may supersede previously definitive actions by taking them to a higher level of righteousness than that which has already been recorded.

Both the Jewish community and the Christian community have tried to take the constitutive statements of the Scriptures and make them "constitutional" by standardizing and canonizing the texts. The fact that this process has not always been smoothly or evenly done, that it has been debated, is a reflection of the seriousness with which the constitutive nature of the text has been taken. The canonical process is basically a deliberative, self-conscious endorsement of the constitutive nature of that which is actually canonized; it has been undertaken dialectically, i.e., by rational debate and by recognized authority authenticating the procedures. As it was stated in the preceding chapter when a person or a community adopts a precedent narrative as its own story, it becomes formative for all those involved.

The narratives which make up the constitutive language of the Bible include the use of other forms of consequential statements. The two which are inexorably bound up in the narratives are bonding language and directive language. This gives to the constitutive narrative two secondary consequential qualities. Because the narratives are about the intimate interaction of God and His chosen people, the sense of bonding is present in the narratives through specifically bonding genre (promises, covenants, vows, etc.) that are not the immediate topic of a given narrative. The constitutive narrative language of the Old and New Testament also includes directive statements, commands, etc., but the narratives themselves are not articulated in commandment form. The inclusion of these two genres within the constitutive narrative language of the Bible carries with it a sense of "oughtness," an imperative quality. It is this imperative quality of the narratives which permits their employment by later users of the text as moral precedents for subsequent generations. The constitutive consequence of the material makes it possible to treat the narratives as having bonding and directive consequences as well.

BONDING STATEMENTS

Bonding statements are statements which are used to establish relationships between two or more persons on an interpersonal level. They shape the status and future of those who are bound together. The consequence of using bonding statements is essentially social. Bonding statements include promises, covenants, wills, adoptions, marriages, legal contracts, etc. Many bonding statements are interpersonal, I- Thou, communications in which two or more persons consciously exchange promises and agree to abide by the process. However, there are bonding events, such as adoption, inheritance, or organizational agreements that take place without some of the parties being conscious of the commitments and status derived from the bonding statement.

The purpose of a bonding statement is to define and secure the future relationship between the parties involved. They are enacted for the sake of stability, whether they are undertaken out of affection or for pragmatic reasons. Bonding statements are authenticated when they are fulfilled, i.e., they are successful if the terms of the bonding are kept. They are fiduciary statements which call on the parties to remain faithful to the terms of the bonding. The faith which they require is more than a belief in the truth or falsity of the statements which are used in the bonding process; it includes remaining faithful to the terms of the bond.

The reliability of the bonding statements on the interpersonal level depends upon the character of those entering into the relationship. Often a bonding event is secured by the community in which it takes place. For example, contracts, trust accounts, guardianships, etc., are not only kept by the parties involved but are regulated and overseen by the community in which they take place to protect the parties in a fiduciary relationship.

The community may require a public ceremony such as a wedding or a recording of a contract to solemnize and give significance to the event.

Bonding statements anticipate the future and attempt to shape it. They are future oriented, and in some religious settings they are eschatological. Insofar as they anticipate the future, they are attempts to define it, if not control it. The content of the statement usually expresses and anticipates a positive ending; bonding statements are essentially hopeful statements. Those who enter bonding statements expect to share in a common destiny or future. Therefore the language carries an element of intimacy, especially when the bonding is entered into self-consciously and willingly. In interpersonal bonding there is a sharing of one's selfhood, a willingness to run the risk of being responsible to and for another person. Because so much is at stake, bonding statements carry an imperative, i.e., they ought to be kept. Although they are not commands themselves, a person is culpable who is unfaithful to the bond which she or he has entered.

In the Bible bonding statements are primarily covenants and promises, although the images of adoption and marriage are also used to illustrate the bond between God and humankind. The covenants and promises which are included in the constitutive narratives of the Bible are definitive of the relationship between God and humankind. They also illustrate the bonding between two or more humans. The record of these bonding events is more than a historical record; they are events which each generation is to reaffirm and keep because their content encompasses those who follow as well as those with whom the covenant and promises were originally made. In the Bible it is incumbent upon those who are inheritors of the bond to remain faithful to the terms of the covenant and promises.

Covenants, like the narrative in which they are embedded, do not remain static. For the Christian there is a super-session of the Old Testament covenant by the covenant made through Jesus Christ. The new covenant entails a higher righteousness, a wider range of persons, and a promise of a more immediate relationship to God for the individual. It entails the presence of God's Spirit in the Church. The symbolic enactments of the Old Testament and New Testament covenants are performed differently, but they both presuppose sincerity and the intention to remain faithful to the bonding relationship. The trust created in the ritual and linguistic enactment of their force is in no way diminished. In both the Abrahamic covenant and the New Testament covenant in Jesus Christ, faithfulness is pivotal to the bonding statements and mandated for future generations. Faithfulness to the bond is the criterion as to whether the bond is made sincerely and honestly. Without intentional faithfulness the bond becomes misspoken, either as a mistake or a fraud, and loses its power and function. Faith is such an important feature of the covenant in Jesus Christ between God and humankind, that it is touted as the grounds of salvation from sin and separation from God.

Expressive statements in the Bible range from ecstasy to despair, from the Song of Solomon to Lamentations. The consequential meaning, the performative functions of the various expressions varies considerably. It would be convenient to say that the expressive statements have the sole purpose of venting the pent-up emotions of the authors (or the reader who identifies with the writer) and allow them to move from the internal world to the external world in a therapeutic outpouring. To some degree this may be part of the function of expressive statements in the Bible, however, expressive language has other consequences for the hearer/reader.

The most numerous and prominent forms of expressive statements in the Bible are not statements of ecstasy and joy but the articulation of Israel's and human frailty. Job, Ecclesiastes, and Lamentations, and sections of the Psalms are expressions of the deepest forms of human suffering, loss, and vulnerability. As expressive language they make overt the writer's covert torment or resignation. They express their writer's inward suffering, loss, anxiety, and sense of God-forsakeness. Some persons might say that their questioning of the goodness of God and their observation on the meaninglessness of life may have the consequential meaning of therapeutic release. However, this conclusion is dangerous in that the statements may very well eventuate in even deeper despair for some readers. What seems to be the most productive consequence of these writings is the reinforcement of human tentativeness, impotence, and total dependence on God. It seems that the consequential meaning for readers, who identify with these texts, is a crisis in which they either embrace the fatalism implied by the writings or accept their vulnerability and dependence on God. Lament for some is the first step toward repentance and transformation. When it is, it does not lose its expressive painfulness, but it becomes a prelude for a return to God.

The inclusion of these forms of expressive language in the Bible gives the reader permission to have these feelings without a sense of guilt; it opens up the possibility of using them in a productive manner. Recognizing that others have spoken and written in these terms helps the readers to realize that they are not alone. It legitimizes their acute feelings and gives them a way to express them without feeling that they have passed completely beyond the providence of God. The description of life without God, or the expression of separation from God's providence in the constitutive narratives, is made existential for the reader. The reader can identify with the writer in his weakness, sinfulness, and sense of abandonment to the powers of darkness.

Expressive language is never objective description, academic debate and dialogue, or disinterested philosophical analysis. It may be misread as such. As Scripture its consequential meaning is personal address. It is not just information about the human condition that needs psychoanalysis. Its meaning is complete when the language is able to uncover the soul, and give it a working place in the world of communication between spirits. Expressive language in Scripture is experience shared in the writing; otherwise, why put it into words for others to read?

The expressive language of joy, its expansiveness, opens the possibility in the reader to happiness. If it is possible for the writer to run the edges of ecstasy, then there is encouragement to the reader to open up his proclivity for real and lasting joy under the providence of God. The awe, solemnness, fear, and seriousness of a defining moment with God, can also be a period of joy and sometime euphoria. The message of the psalm:

> But let all who take refuge in Thee
> rejoice,
> let them ever sing for joy;
> and do Thou defend them,
> that those who love Thy name
> may exult in Thee.
> For Thou dost bless the righteous,

O Lord;
Thou dost cover him with favor
as with a shield.
(Ps.5:11-12)

The human condition with God has its times of deep distress, but also high joy.

The consequential meaning of expressive texts such as the Song of Solomon is more than the poetic form of ecstatic romance. They raise the possibility of bonding being more than mere agreements and covenants. Such statements suggest that genuine bonding becomes a thirst, a longing, which is not satisfied with the formal process of covenanting, but seeks an ecstatic union with the "other" who has become the beloved.

THE CHOICE OF POSSIBILITIES

Exalting language always carries with it an expressive element, but its consequential meaning or performative function is to prioritize that which is important. Praising, honoring, glorifying, worshipping, magnifying, and extolling raise that which is exalted to a place of preeminence. It reinforces both the social and individual significance of that which is exalted. It raises it from the mundane and commonplace and makes it of utmost importance.

In worship exalting language moves its object out of the profane into the realm of the holy. It differentiates that which is worthy from that which is common and unworthy. Praise magnifies its object, i.e., gives it magnitude, and brings it to the foreground of one's consciousness. It underwrites the sense of awe and wonder with which one is conscious of that which excels in greatness, strength, goodness, knowledge, and beauty.

The language of exaltation tends toward hyperbole and overstatement because it cannot represent its object in ordinary referential terms. Sometimes exalting language is expressed in analogy or metaphor because our ordinary referential meaning is too pedestrian; it is not rich enough in significance to carry out the performative function of elevating the subject. Often exalting language is expansive, poetic, and expresses itself in song and dance. We see it in the narrative of David dancing before the Ark

(II Sam. 6:14), in Hanna's song (I Sam. 2:1-10), and in Mary's response to the angel (Lk.1:46-55). It runs throughout the Psalter, in the visions of the prophets and in the images of the Book of Revelation.

The performative outcome of praise is not something which happens to everyone who hears or reads the words, but to those who are receptive to the prioritization of that which is exalted. When the consequential meaning is appropriated by the hearer or reader, the object or person being praised become charged with importance. The poetry and imagery have a surplus of significance which is visceral, i.e., they "move" us.

The language of the second chapter of Philippians gives us a good illustration of exalting language,

> Therefore God has highly exalted Him and bestowed on Him the name which is above every name, that at the name of Jesus every knee shall bow in heaven and earth and under the earth, and every tongue confess that Jesus Christ is Lord, to the glory of God the Father (Phil. 2:9-13).

The language gives Jesus a preeminence which amounts to a metaphysical status. The simple statement "Jesus is Lord," or the appellation "Lord," both recognize the primary place of Jesus Messiah in the lives of those who utter the phrases with sincerity. The flip side of every statement of worship, praise, or honor is the acceptance of the inferior role to that which is exalted. Jesus' exaltation is grounds for obedience to him. The consequential meaning of the passage in Philippians 2:12-13 is both exalting and directing.

One of the functions of exalting language is to reinforce the priorities set out in the constitutive language which makes up the community. By glorifying or magnifying the features of one's constitutive language it elevates the significance of that which is definitive in one's life by celebrating it. Celebration incorporates an exuberance and abandonment before that which is worthy.

E. TRANSFORMING STATEMENTS

Transformational language is language which initiates change in the very nature of the hearer or reader. The consequence of using the language is to become what one is not, or to return to what one once was. The language of transformation may come about religiously from an external source such a preaching or the reading of a text in which God acts through the Spirit to change one's constitutive make up; it may come from within as something one utters, such as a vow, that re-centers one's life. What ever the source, transforming language changes the character of that which is addressed by it.

The goal of most prophetic preaching is to bring about a transformation in the hearer or reader. In voicing the word of God the prophet's warnings and promises are more than directives and predictions; they are used to bring about change in the hearer. The accusations and promises have a performative force. The prophet is not merely announcing the future, but he is creating the future as he declares the Word of God (See the authenticating criteria for a true prophet in chapter III).

The prophet's use of constitutive and covenant language in his call to return to God take on the force of reconstituting that language in the consciousness of the hearer/reader. It is used to reform, to recreate the hearer/reader in his/her very being and eventuates in actions which reflect God's righteousness. It is written in I Samuel 10 that after Samuel had anointed Saul as king of Israel he predicted that Saul would become a prophet:

> When he turned his back to leave Samuel, God gave him another heart; and all these signs came to pass that day. When they came to Gibeah behold a band of prophets met him; and the spirit of God came mightily upon him, and he prophesied among them. And when all who knew him before saw how he prophesied with the prophets, the people said to one another, "What has come over the son of Kish? Is Saul also among the prophets?" And a man of the place answered, "And who is their father?" Therefore it became a proverb, "Is Saul among the prophets?" When he had finished prophesying, he came to a high place. (I Sam. 10:9-13).

The address of transformational language is not limited to individuals, but often is intended for the community as a whole. The community is called to remember in order than they may be "re-minded," i.e., their consciousness reshaped. The society itself is to be reshaped into a community of righteousness, justice, and mercy that reflects the fact that it is

God's chosen people.

> For your Maker is your husband, the Lord of host is his name; and
> the Holy One of Israel is your Redeemer, the God of the whole earth
> he is called. For the Lord has called you like a wife forsaken and
> grieved in spirit, like a wife of youth when she is cast off, says your
> God. For a brief moment I forsook you, but with great compassion
> I will gather you. In overflowing wrath for a moment I hid my face
> from you, but with everlasting love I will have compassion on you,
> say the Lord, your Redeemer (Isa. 54: 5-8).

Where the community has become idolatrous it is to return to its constitutive origin and covenant commitment as God's own people. The transformational language of the prophets is meant to have an effect on the fundamental structure of the society to reconstitute it.

A prophet's transformational message is never just delivered and left like a package on the doorstep; it is a summons delivered in person, when the prophet speaks the Word of God. It is God who addresses the hearer/reader directly in an I-Thou manner. The speech carries the weight of direct charismatic dialogue. It is charismatic in that it is Spirit directly addressing spirit. Its consequences always involve more than the exchange of words; it involves interpersonal reactions. It is one thing to ignore someone's words, and another thing to ignore the person. The words are the medium through which spirits are opened and closed to one another, where acceptance or rejection, dominion or submission, union or separation are mediated through discourse.

Whether it is Hosea's metaphorical narrative of God's love or Amos's declaration of God's righteousness, both forms of speech call for repentance (return), not simply remorse. The preaching of Stephen in Acts was not merely a recitation of Israel's history and Jesus' place in God's providence, but a call for a radical change – the transformation of the constitutive structure of the leadership of the Jewish community (Acts 6:6-7:58). The response to it cannot be understood unless one accepts that it was a bold personal affront which was both an accusation and a promise of the messianic future. It certainly cannot be seen merely as a referential statement. The accusations, judgment, and promises of the prophet may be both correct and fulfilled, but the hearer is not automatically transformed by the words unless there is assimilation. Transformational language is not mechanical or magic; it requires being taken to heart. God's word is not irresistible. The prophet's word is not impugned by those who resist it. It is impugned if the judgment or promise that the prophet states does not come to pass.

Among statements which are comforting are those which are directed toward specific events of sorrow and grief. There are other statements which give assurance, provide hope, inspire strength, reaffirm promises, encourage perseverance, and confirm the caring presence of another person. The prophetic books and Pastoral Epistles are replete with these types of statements.

In order for comforting statements to achieve their end, they must be appropriated; and they must be believable. There is not much comfort in words which do not acknowledge the pain and suffering of the person being comforted. Nor is there much comfort in a Pollyanna approach to grief and loss. The rules for comforting require that the comforter enter the suffering of the person who is being consoled and speak, or communicate with silence, empathically. A comforter must enter reverently into the holy of holies of the sufferer, and there wait. While waiting the comforter must wait on, serve the sufferer. The sufferer sets the agenda, not the comforter. Note the failure of Job's friends to even come near to dealing with his suffering. Patience and willingness to serve the sufferer are essential ingredients for the use of the language of comforting just as sincerity is built into the rules of promise making.

The consequential meaning of comforting language may be given without there being a crisis or loss. Blessings are pronounced on the joyful and the sorrowing. They carry the weight of authority. It may be the authority of the speaker or it may be the authority of someone who represents the authority. Blessing always comes from a source of strength; they impart strength. They are a grant, a favor, bestowed by the giver. They emerge from love or goodwill toward the person being blessed. In many cases the act is consigning the blessed to God for God's keeping. To bless some one is presumptuous in that it assumes that the giver has the power and authority to pronounce the blessing. True blessings flow from great spiritual strength that is recognized and appreciated by the recipient.

In our ordinary speech we know how to hurt other people with words; we know how to curse. There is very little in our daily speech which is recognized as blessing or enhancing language. We have a trove of four letter words in our daily vocabulary, which we use to condemn, damn, name, or demean others, but there is no comparable set of words for enhancing, strengthening, blessing, or enabling except possibly the phrase, "I love you."

The Bible, on the other hand, has numerous blessing statements which can be used to enhance the life of a recipient. One of the better known blessings is God's instruction to Moses to have Aaron and his sons bless Israel by saying, "The Lord bless you and keep you; the Lord make his face to shine upon you, and be gracious to you, and give you peace" (Numbers 6:24-26). The Aaronic blessing is explained in terms of its consequential meaning. "So that they put my name upon the people of Israel, and I will bless them" (Numbers 6:27).

Blessings, like promises, are not descriptive language, but acts which shape and envision the future of the recipient. Blessings are fulfilled. A blessing is not an agreement or a binding promise; it is bestowed as a gift. When Jesus gives the beatitudes in Matthew's Gospel, they are declarations of the future for those who are poor in spirit, those who mourn, the meek, those who hunger and thirst for righteousness, the merciful, the pure in heart, the peacemakers, and those who are persecuted for righteousness sake. Blessings are grounds for hope.

The ending of the book of Jude is interesting because it incorporates Jude's injunction to the reader about the future.

> But you, beloved, build yourselves up on your holy faith; pray in the Holy Spirit; keep yourselves in the love of God; wait for the mercy of our Lord Jesus Christ unto eternal life. And convince some who doubt; save some, by snatching them out of the fire; on some have mercy with fear, hating even the garment spotted by the flesh (Jude 1:20-23).

The writer ends those injunctions with a benediction which is both an act of praise and a blessing.

> Now unto him who is able to keep you from falling and to present
> you without blemish before the presence of his glory with rejoicing,
> to the only God, our Savior through Jesus Christ our Lord, be glory,
> majesty, dominion, and authority, before all time and now and
> forever, Amen (Jude 1:24-25).

The consequential uses of language in the Bible have not been ex-
hausted in the analysis above; nor has any one of the uses mentioned been
explored fully. An attempt has been made to differentiate a number of
forms of consequential meaning and show that interpretation is basic to
the full understanding of the given text. Looking at a biblical text for its
referential meaning alone is simply not adequate. Information which is
laid down in referential meaning always has consequential meaning, even
if the meaning is nothing more than to enlighten the reader.

We have not addressed numerous issues. Given that certain statements
have consequences, what needs to be considered when the significance
of those statements changes? How is the consequential meaning of a text
changed in the process of super-session? In looking at the changes in the
meaning or understanding of a text, are there mechanisms and criteria for
those changes that can be drawn from the Bible that determine how those
changes are to be understood? If there are changes in understanding one's
relationship with God and one's fellow human beings in the subsequent
life of the Church, what criteria for those changes can be drawn from the
Bible itself?

If one is to read the Bible as Christian Scripture, it is totally inade-
quate to read it only on the referential level. Interpreting the Bible in terms
of its referential accuracy is to read the Bible as though it has not depth
of significance or consequence, which is to misread the text altogether.
The Historical Critical method treats language as if it has only referential
meaning and no other. It has provided numerous insights, but it is only one
dimension of the text, and one that becomes misleading if it is not aug-

mented by the significance of that text and the consequence it has for the readers. The reader of the Bible must learn to dialogue with the text, i.e., treat it as the communication of spirits with one another. Communication is always multi-layered between persons and persons, between spirits and persons. In any communication between persons there is always far more going on than is stated in referential terms. It is no wonder that when the Bible is read only for its referential meaning eventually its religious meaning goes transparent to the reader. Nothing has been communicated except the sterile image of representational language. Pure objectivity is poor interpersonal communication. It fails to deal with the complexity of genuine communication between people, much less that between God and humankind.

ENDNOTES

---

[1] J.L. Austin, How to Do Things With Words, Ed. by J.O. Urmson, Oxford, Oxford University Press, 1970..

[2] H. Wheeler Robinson, Inspiration and Revelation in the Old Testament, Oxford, At The Clarendon Press, 1946, Pp. 170-172.

[3] All language usage has consequential meaning; But not everything is that is said is deliberately thought through or is a conscious choice. When we use certain language genre and follow the community's language rules with regard to them, we often do so without deliberation. We often greet one another, we inform one another, we question one another, we advise one another, etc., without self consciously doing so. It is a very much like playing the piano; we do not think about where to place our fingers on the keyboard when we are following the score. We previously learned how to achieve this consequence. When we learn a language we habituate the patterns and behavior of that language. What produces the proper consequences is whether or not we follow the rules, not necessarily our consciousness through out the process.

[4] Peter Berger, The Sacred Canopy, New York, Doubleday, 1967: Clifford Geertz, The Interpretation of Culture, New York, Basic Books, 1973.

[5] George Linbeck, The Nature of Doctrine, Philadelphia, Westminster Press, 1984, p. 13.

ABOUT THE AUTHOR

James H, Ware Jr. was born in Shanghai, China of missionary parents. He received his B.A. and M.A. degrees from Baylor University and his B.D. from Southern Baptist Theological Seminary. Duke University granted him his Ph.D.

At Clemson University, University of Central Arkansas, and Austin College he taught Asian Religions, the Philosophy of Language, Biblical Studies, Hermeneutics, and the History of Philosophy. Through out his academic career he has pastored numerous churches.

Dr. Ware's first two books were study guides to Chinese and Korean Religions published by Yale Divinity School Press. His third work, Not With Word of Wisdom, dealt with performative language and liturgy. In 2001 he published Heart Sing, which consists of 350 morning prayers of praise and thanksgiving.

Following retirement from Austin College he has served as Parish Associate at Gulf Breeze Presbyterian Church and has been dealing with biblical hermeneutics and the life of the Church.

The Southwest Commission on Religious Studies presented him the John Gammie Distinguished Scholar's Award in 1994-5. Previously he received a post doctoral award from the Fund for the Study of the World Great Religions and spend six months at the University of Hong Kong and six months at the University of Chicago.